Wedding Officiant Manual

𝔑orth 𝔖hore 𝔘niversal 𝔈hurch
Wedding Officiant Manual

The Definitive How-to Guide on Conducting
Remarkable Marriage Ceremonies

Rodney Krafka

Copyright © 2020 by NSUC

Seattle WA, USA

All Rights Reserved

North Shore Universal Church
Publications & Education Dept.
5901 20th Ave NW,
Suite 8
Seattle WA, 98107, USA

www.OrdainMinister.com

Dedication

This book is dedicated to Dr. Martin Luther King Jr.

As a minister, leader, civil rights activist, author, and Nobel Peace Prize recipient, Dr. King is known as one of the greatest communicators of all time. Through him and his work we are provided an amazing example for how to maintain integrity through adversity for the betterment of humanity. He held onto truth and stood up for what was right.

Discover more about Dr. King's life of service and sacrifice from The King Center https://thekingcenter.org/about-dr-king/.

Quotes from Dr. Martin Luther King Jr.[1]

"Faith is taking the first step even when you can't see the whole staircase."

"Use me, God. Show me how to take who I am, who I want to be, and what I can do, and use it for a purpose greater than myself."

"Not everybody can be famous but everybody can be great, because greatness is determined by service... You only need a heart full of grace and a soul generated by love."

"The time is always right to do the right thing."

---

[1] (Reprinted from: https://www.crosswalk.com/faith/spiritual-life/inspiring-quotes/31-powerful-quotes-by-dr-martin-luther-king-jr.html)

Table of Contents

Introduction 1
   Guide to this Book 3
Ten Step Outline for Officiating a Wedding 8
   1. Get Ordained 8
   2. Contact the County Courthouse 9
      County Courthouse Checklist 9
   3. Create a Timeline 11
   4. Get Organized 13
   5. Discuss the Couple's Vision for the Ceremony 14
      Ceremony Preparation Interview Questions 16
   6. Write the Ceremony 17
   7. Finishing the Vows and Completing the Script Text. 18
   8. Practice the Ceremony 19
   9. Deliver the Ceremony 21
      Non-Verbal Tips for Being an Engaging Officiant: 21
   10. Sign the Marriage Certificate 25
NSUC Comprehensive Wedding Ceremony Script 27
   Guide to the NSUC Comprehensive Wedding Ceremony Script 27
   Wedding Script Template 31
      WELCOMING 31
      PROCESSION 31
      OPENING WORDS 31
   Opening Poem: "To See the Sun" (E. E. Cummings) 32
   QUERY 34
   BLESSINGS 35
   READINGS 37

Poem: "How do I Love Thee" (Elizabeth Barrett Brownig) 37
Reading from: The Prophet (Khalil Gibran) 38
Reading from: 1st Corinthians: 13; verses 4-13 40
INTRODUCTION TO THE VOWS 41
VOWS 42
INTRODUCTION TO THE RING VOWS 44
RING VOWS 46
RING CEREMONY AFFIRMATION 47
UNITY CEREMONY 48
    Candle 48
    Sand 49
    Rose 50
    Water 51
SIGNING OF THE MARRIAGE REGISTER AND LICENSE 53
MEDITATION OR PRAYER 53
PRONOUNCEMENT 56
CLOSING WORDS 57
SPEAKING TO THE CHILDREN 59
PRESENTATION 60

Supplemental Readings 61
    Wedding Prayer by Robert Louis Stevenson 61
    Wedding Blessing by his holiness the 14th Dalai Lama 62
    "Blessing of the Hands" by Unknown 63
    "What is Love" by Unknown 63
    Apache Wedding Blessing 64

Wedding Rehearsal and Processional Primer 65
    Running the Rehearsal and Practicing the Processional 67
    Processional, Recessional, & Position Assignment Diagram 71
    Variations in Wedding Processions 72

Breaking with Tradition (but keeping the rehearsal dinner).74
Resources for Emotional and Psychological Support **75**
   Readings for Emotional and Psychological Encouragement 78
   Encouraging Scriptures 82
   Helpful Aphorisms 83
   Gratitude is the path to the best actualization of life. 84
   Four Rules for Living, by Dr. Wayne Dyer 84
   Ten Stress Management Techniques, by Dr. Wayne Dyer ... 88
State Laws at a Glance **96**
   Alabama Code 96
   Alaska Code 97
   Arizona Revised Statutes 98
   Arkansas Code 98
   California Law - Family Code 99
   Colorado Revised Statutes 101
   Connecticut General Statutes 102
   Delaware Code 103
   Florida Statutes 104
   Georgia Code Annotated 105
   Hawaii Revised Statutes 106
   Idaho Statutes 106
   Illinois Compiled Statutes 107
   Indiana Code 108
   Iowa Code 109
   Kansas Statutes 109
   Kentucky Revised Statutes 110
   Louisiana Revised Statutes 111
   Maine Revised Statutes 111
   Maryland Code - Family Law 112
   Massachusetts General Laws 114
   Michigan Compiled Laws 115

Minnesota Code	117
Mississippi Code	117
Missouri Revised Statutes	118
Montana Code Annotated	119
Nebraska Revised Statutes	120
Nevada Revised Statutes	120
New Hampshire Statutes	122
New Jersey Permanent Statutes	123
New Mexico Statutes Annotated	124
New York Law Code	124
North Carolina General Statutes	127
North Dakota Century Code	127
Ohio Revised Code	128
Oklahoma Statutes	128
Oregon Revised Statutes	130
Pennsylvania Consolidated Statutes	130
Rhode Island General Laws	132
South Carolina Code of Laws	133
South Dakota Codified Laws	134
Tennessee Code	134
Texas Statutes	137
Utah Code	138
Vermont Statutes	139
Virginia Law Code	140
Washington Law Code	141
Washington DC Code	141
West Virginia Code	143
Wisconsin Statutes	145
Wyoming Code	146

Wedding Officiant Manual

Introduction

Congratulations, it is an honor to be asked to conduct a wedding. This should make clear to you the very high level of esteem and respect that the couple has for you in asking you to help them make their marital commitment official. You will want to give them a respectable ceremony that they can reflect upon with pride and happiness. While this is a serious position that includes a high level of responsibility, they would not have asked you if they were not convinced that you would perform remarkably and do an overall excellent job.

You may wonder what your role entails...

The diverse legal roles a wedding officiant will play vary across state lines within the U.S. From a legal perspective, the most important thing is that with your signature, you commit that you have found no reason to object to the marriage. It means that, as the officiant, you understand that those getting married have obeyed all laws in doing so, that there are no legal hindrances (such as age or already being married), and that everything is in order.

The signature is also a testament that you're a witness to the sharing of vows and pronounce them as marriage partners before other witnesses. In some states, the officiant also needs to file and complete the paperwork after the ceremony for the vital records office and make document copies to be sent to the groom and bride as keepsakes.

The officiant is also a part of the wedding planning process. The couple might want a personalized ceremony and a somewhat unique wedding, therefore you need to be alerted to prepare accordingly.

The officient also appears at the wedding rehearsal party or dinner and has the role of supervising the ceremony and often meeting other suggested requests. Rehearsals are generally great fun, practicing the ceremony gives the couple the opportunity to make final adjustments to the ceremony.

And of course, the officiant conducts the wedding ceremony itself. As an ordained minister, you will open and close the entire wedding, from the first step of the processional to the last words of presenting the couple and signing the license, a true master of ceremonies. Every part of this journey is honorable, memorable and rewarding. With composed excitement and a well-practiced ceremony script, you will be a great leader for the couple as they navigate this joyous and wonderful day.

Planning their wedding ceremony is a happy task. It is also a task to be approached thoughtfully, for it is a ceremony in which the couple will seek to express their deepest convictions about their relationship and about the marriage they intend to build together.

It's also worth noting that the officiant's duties can begin way before the wedding date. After you're ordained, these duties may include coordinating with state and local government agencies in order to ascertain the steps necessary to cover all legal requirements. These first steps are required to legally ground your ministry so that you act in an official and legally recognized capacity. You will also be in a position to help guide or assist the couple as they coordinate with these government agencies about marriage licensing documents and timelines.

North Shore Universal Church

You will be participating in a great adventure. Use this book to understand your obligations even if you have limited exposure to wedding processes. And importantly, please remember to enjoy the ride as you assist the couple in creating the best wedding possible.

Guide to this Book

Welcome to the Third Revised Edition of our North Shore Universal Church (NSUC) Minister's Wedding Manual. We are happy to have you with us.

This book has five main parts:

1. Our NSUC Comprehensive Wedding Script;
2. Our Wedding Rehearsal and Processional Primer;
3. Our Ten Step Outline for Officiating a Wedding;
4. Our Pocket State Law Reference; and,
5. Our Resources for Emotional and Psychological Support.

The core of this book is our **North Shore Universal Church Comprehensive Wedding Script**, which will help you customize the best wedding ceremony given your unique needs. We also include several of the most prominent and expressive readings for weddings. These readings can be supplemented into the text of any personalized script entirely at your discretion.

There are a great many words to choose from throughout our NSUC Comprehensive Script, and we expect you'll take what you need and leave the rest. The Script's text itself generally contains a few interchangeable versions for each section of the wedding ceremony. The couple may also include materials and symbols which have personal meaning for them, perhaps from different religious traditions. Or they may want to include children, friends or family members as participants in the ceremony. Our wedding script allows for all of this, and has multiple interchangeable text components for each part of the ceremony that you and the couple can build together. You may change, combine, or add to these text components as you see fit when planning the ceremony.

After the conclusion of our NSUC Script, we have included five additional readings, known for their popularity. You can supplement your customized wedding script with any or all of these readings at any point. Altogether, we make nine readings available in this manual, chosen for their poignancy and timelessness.

In addition to the Comprehensive Script, we have included our **Wedding Rehearsal and Processional Primer**. Officiant duties can vary, and sometimes include responsibilities at the rehearsal. We include this Primer in case your duties start to expand. But regardless of whether you're expected to speak at the rehearsal, we want you to know what to expect. There can be some initial confusion during the wedding rehearsal and the designations within the processional. Our primer takes out all of the guess work and helps you focus on organizing people and space in the most efficient manner should these obligations fall onto your shoulders.

Within our Rehearsal and Processional Primer, we have included our "Processional, Recessional and Position Assignment Diagram." This map-like layout shows where everyone should stand and indicates their ordering within both the processional and recessional walks. In addition to the conventional standards described through the diagram, we have also included four alternatives in our "Variations in Wedding Processionals" which can be found at the end of the chapter.

We have also included an expansive chapter on state marriage laws in our **Pocket State Law Reference**. This resource will help identify who can, and under what circumstances, officiate a marriage ceremony. Many weddings are destination events, so we provide this portable hard-copy, quick reference on the most relevant state marriage laws. Every state is listed in alphabetical order and can be located directly through our Table of Contents above. For each state we include the most relevant section describing who can officiate weddings. Online we have the complete catalogue of all marriage laws for each state underneath the "Resources" tab on our organization's home page at: **OrdainMinister.com**.

For a spot reference, use our Pocket Law Reference below. And for complete marriage laws on a state-by-state basis, visit our complete State Law Library online at: **https://ordainminister.com/state-marriage-laws/**. Between these two resources, you should always have the information you need to understand what makes a marriage official.

In addition to the Script, Primer, and Pocket Law Reference, we have also included our trusted procedural resource: **Ten Step Outline for Officiating a Wedding**. Think of this highly detailed chapter as your roadmap for this entire legal and procedural process as you navigate your role and obligations, from start to end.

In particular, our Ten Step Outline includes our "County Courthouse Checklist" which can be a critical resource when speaking with government authorities at the courthouse. It's good to have some questions in hand as a starting point, and this checklist provides a good structure for your inquiry.

Wedding Officiant Manual

Our Ten Step Outline includes another list composed of twelve questions you can use to interview the couple, our "Ceremony Preparation Interview Questions." This checklist itemizes the best questions to ask the couple to help you get to know them better both personally, as well as what drew them together. This improved understanding of the couple will help you write a more personalized script, and you can insert the most relevant parts of their story into our comprehensive script template below.

Also included in the Ten Step Outline is a brief discussion about performance, delivery and our list of "Non-verbal Tips for Being an Engaging Officiant."

As the wedding day unfolds, there may be a few surprises. But if you hold tight to our Ten Step Officiation guidelines, and follow each of the steps outlined, you will not overlook any necessary procedural requirement as you carry out your duties to officiate an enjoyable, memorable, and fully legal wedding.

Altogether, this book is a great resource for any wedding officiant. We have included everything that you will need to conduct weddings anywhere in the United States: our NSUC Comprehensive Wedding Script, our Wedding Rehearsal and Processional Primer, our Ten Steps for Officiating a Wedding, our Pocket State Law Reference, and a lot more.

Lastly, we have included a brief section on **Resources for Emotional and Psychological Support**. As the presiding minister, people may be reaching out to you for a variety of reasons, including the couple, but perhaps any of the wedding party or attendants. Weddings can bring out a lot of emotions, and some people may want some manner of advice or to speak with you about some of the problems they've encountered in life. We want to make available these messages on positivity and gratitude, so that they are more deliverable to whoever may find themselves in need.

By making good use of the resources in this book, you will perform your function honorably, and remind everyone why you were entrusted to help ensure a great wedding – an event that will be made all the more memorable with your wise and thoughtful contributions.

Ten Step Outline for Officiating a Wedding

1. Get Ordained

If you're not already ordained, you'll most likely need to get this done. There are two types of authorities that can officiate a wedding: 1) civil; and, 2) religious. Civil authorities include judges, magistrates, notary publics, and various government officials. Religious authorities include church clergy, ministers, rabbis, deacons, priests, and anyone ordained by a religious organization for the purpose of marrying two people. These ordained authorities are not bound to perform a religious ceremony, but can also choose to conduct secularized, civil ceremonies.

If you are not a designated civil authority, then your only option to perform marriage ceremonies is to act as an ordained religious authority. Our organization, North Shore Universal Church, offers ordainments accepted by all 50 state governments (plus Washington D.C.). If you haven't gotten ordained, you can get ordained online with us now. We will ordain you for no cost. Please check out our website and start the ordination process at **www.OrdainMinister.com**.

Some states have registration requirements, including waiting periods which could commence either after your ordination, or after you register as an NSUC minister with the appropriate state agency (if applicable). To forestall any confusion, you should be ordained ASAP before moving to step two of this outline.

2. Contact the County Courthouse

Contact the county courthouse where you will perform the wedding and figure out exactly what you will need to conduct a legal ceremony. Use the following checklist when communicating with those local authorities:

County Courthouse Checklist

- Ask specifically about how to get a Marriage License. If necessary, ask to speak to the Bureau/Office of Vital Statistics.
- Are there any deadlines you should be aware of, either before or after the marriage license is signed?
- Are there any waiting periods for the marriage license to become effective?
- Is there a specific window of time within which the marriage license is valid?
- Is there any documentation you need to provide the state before or after the wedding?
- Is there any registration that you may need to do with the state as a minister of NSUC church?
- Are there any waiting periods or procedures for you as a minister after you register your ministry (if necessary)?
- Are there any fees that might need to be paid by anyone?

The couple should have already filed for the marriage license prior to the wedding date. They will pick it up and present the blank license to you along with detailed state and county-specific instructions on how to fill it out, along with any relevant timelines, and the process for returning a completed license. Even though they should give you these instructions and timelines, you should also research this information directly yourself so that you know it is correct. It is your obligation as an ordained minister of NSUC to conduct a legal wedding – so you should call the county where the wedding will be performed and acquire all the necessary information and paperwork.

The couple should be able to inform you of the location where the wedding will be performed. Look up this location on the internet and find out the phone number for the county clerk where the wedding will be located. Call this number and save this number for quick access in the future. Be conscious of time-zone changes in calling across the country.

Look into the laws of the state and county where the couple will be having the ceremony and familiarize yourself with any state requirements you'll need in order to conduct the wedding. Do you need specific documentation to include with their marriage license such as a "Letter of Good Standing" with the church? Or are they saying "I do" in one of the few parts of the country where the couple can self-solemnize their own marriage (Wisconsin, Colorado, parts of Pennsylvania, and the District of Columbia), allowing you to serve a symbolic role without any legal requirements?

Will you be required to register your ministry with the NSUC with the state you will be officiating in? Some states have this requirement, including: Arkansas, Hawaii, Louisiana, Massachusetts, Minnesota, Nevada, New Hampshire, New York, Ohio, Oklahoma, Puerto Rico, Vermont, Virginia, West Virginia, and Washington D.C. Therefore, ask the county clerk if there is any preliminary registration necessary to ground your ministry in the state before you conduct the wedding. Collect other key information, such as how long your ordination will be valid, or if you have to have your ordination established for a certain period of time before you can perform the ceremony legally.

You should try to have all of this done at least 6 weeks in advance if possible, as you might need to leave a little time to get something mailed or filed if an oversight occurs. Getting the proper paperwork for the state where you're conducting the wedding is not usually a difficult process, but it's best to figure these things out far in advance so there are no surprises.

Remember: The most efficient way to get answers is to call the county clerk at the marriage/vital records office the clerk can inform you about exactly what you'll be required to have. Just ask the clerk exactly what you will need.

3. Create a Timeline

Dates and times are important with establishing marital unions, and all states have different laws governing the window of time during which the marriage license is valid and can be signed. For example, in Washington State, there is a 3-day wait period until the license is valid, whereupon the license is active for 60 days, and after it's signed it must be returned within 30 days. All of these deadlines are significant, and the marriage couple will need to figure out exactly what they are responsible for. You can check state marriage laws in our data base, and/or call the relevant county courthouse directly.

Once you've figured out all the dates, deadlines and time-frames – write this all down. Mark up a calendar or set reminders to show when you need to have your documents and fees submitted, and when you need to have the couple's marriage license turned in.

It is easy to take things for granted or to assume that "things will take care of themselves." Similarly, you may want to rely on the couple to tell you the timelines. But be conscious that the couple is also relying on you as the officiant to understand the process that you are ushering them through. You are, after all, the presiding authority on marriage laws at their wedding ceremony.

Create a timeline or a calendar as either a physical document or as an e-document online. You can create shareable online documents through Google on their website at **www.google.com/docs.** Creating and sharing these documents online is super easy. Everyone will be able to add to and edit them remotely from their homes, which can be an amazing resource to literally "get everyone on the same page." Give access to the online document, or a copy of the physical timeline, to the couple, because they should have this information as well. But fundamentally, this timeline is for you. This is your reference so that all important dates are respected and so that no oversights or missed deadlines occur.

4. Get Organized

Now that you have your timeline, make sure to store it safely so that you don't have to redo your work. Online documents are easy to access and share, but you will also be working with some physical documents, including a signed marriage certificate, as well as any documents that you may have received from the clerk, such as instructions specific to that county and state.

It is helpful to have a specifically designated binder or folder where you can keep track of any paperwork you're acquiring, along with your notes and the ceremony script that you and the couple are writing together. Staying organized is paramount, especially for an important event like a wedding. Please don't underestimate the real value a single binder can bring to your ministry.

Lastly, on the day of the ceremony, you will want to make sure that if you use electronic devices like iPads and/or any use of cloud storage – please allow for network coverage lapses or device failure. Please make sure you are not depending on something that may not be available on the day of the wedding. It is always a good idea to have a hard copy of any key information immediately available just in case it becomes necessary.

In particular, make sure you have a hard-copy, paper version of your wedding script available on the wedding day. Nothing should stop you from conducting a dynamic and impressive ceremony (including device failure).

5. Discuss the Couple's Vision for the Ceremony

You will want to work closely with the couple, maintaining good communication with them to best ensure that they are happy with their wedding ceremony. You will need to meet with the couple at least once before the wedding to make sure you have the same understandings about all important matters. Prior to this meeting, you should have already begun to work through some of your responsibilities. When you sit down with the couple, you should already have a good understanding of the local process and requirements.

Sit down and walk through the ceremony outline with the couple, as each will want something different. With religious ceremonies, there's a reasonably set pattern and format, but with secular weddings, the couple sometimes wants to throw out the entire playbook. It's very important to talk to them upfront so you can understand their vision for the ceremony.

Ideally, you should meet with them two to four months prior to the wedding. This timeframe gives you plenty of time to plan, but not enough that major changes will occur. At this meeting, walk through their answers to our questionnaire checklist below. As an officiant, your goal is to make this ceremony deeply personal. Even if you're newly acquainted to either or both of the couple, you want the ceremony to feel like you've all known each other for years. Use this meeting to try to understand their relationship and why they care about each other.

North Shore Universal Church

Spend time going over the details of the ceremony. If you have any previous experience with weddings, you can offer to help the couple with other day-of details, such as the order of the processional, what a bride should do with her bouquet, procedures with the ringbearer, etc. Also, take this time to ask how your voice will be amplified. Unless it is an intimate wedding (fewer than 20 guests), <u>you will need a microphone of some kind for the ceremony</u>.

This meeting should last about 45 minutes to an hour, depending on how much the couple needs to discuss.

When you meet with the couple, ask them specific questions about themselves and their intended ceremony. These questions could include the following:

Ceremony Preparation Interview Questions

1. Will the couple write their own vows?

2. Why did they choose the designated wedding location?

3. What rituals will they include?

4. What will they be wearing and/or carrying?

5. What (if any) role will religion play in the ceremony?

6. To what extent should the officiant use any humor?

7. Are there any jokes or anecdotes that the couple think you as the officiant should tell?

8. How did the couple meet? How did the proposal occur?

9. What other stories might help shape the ceremony?

10. What role (if any) will any family or friends play in the ceremony?

11. Will there be a honeymoon or anything else to announce?

12. What elements are most important to incorporate into the ceremony?

North Shore Universal Church

6. Write the Ceremony

If you are either a friend or family to the couple, then you're in a unique position to create a moving, poignant, and richly memorable wedding ceremony. But even if you've only known them for a short period of time, you will still have sufficient information to craft a warm and personal ceremony. After your interview with the couple, you'll have a clear understanding of what they are going for, and you can then start writing an introduction and putting together the text that will surround the readings, exchange of vows, exchange of rings and the pronouncement of marriage!

Ideally, the couple will participate directly with you in the writing of the wedding script. But if they leave you to do this by yourself, you should none-the-less be fully equipped given our comprehensive script template below. You can read the whole thing as it is presently formatted, and you can also freely add to it or take away as you see fit.

As you write the ceremony, infuse it with positive and happy stories about the couple and heartfelt sentiment. Jokes can be great, but don't take it too far. Everybody likes to have a laugh, but remember, this is a wedding. Save your best jokes for the wedding toasts. You don't want to do anything that takes away from the overall importance of the actual wedding occasion.

Officiating a wedding can make a person fell at least a little pressure to say something wise and meaningful about marriage, but this might not be the reason you were even asked. Wedding attendants may have limited appetite for grandiose perspectives. Sometimes just telling a few stories from folks who are dear to the couple makes it all much easier and enjoyable. Alternatively, some ceremony venues are quite composed and elaborate, and people might expect a few extra words to respect and compliment all the other preparations. Ultimately, the ceremony you write should reflect the two people standing in front of you, whether that means it should be silly and lighthearted, or serious and literary.

Email the couple's friends and family members for inspiration. If you're being asked to officiate, you probably know the couple well, but that's only one view of them. So ask around to others who are close to them for funny anecdotes, nostalgic tidbits and inspiration. Here are a few conversation starters: How do you know the couple? What are your favorite memories of them? What do they love about each other? What are their favorite qualities (and pet peeves) about each other? What, in your eyes, makes them click? What do they as a couple bring to the world?

7. Finishing the Vows and Completing the Script Text.

As you complete your customized your wedding script, please briefly consult the couple again. A phone call is ok for this follow-up conversation. See if they have had any new thoughts or matured ideas about their own ambitions for the wedding script. It is generally a good idea to give them at least one follow-up conversation after your initial meeting to see if they have changed their mind in any way, or perhaps evolved in a particular direction. You should show them what you have written, and you should pay particular attention to the vows.

The vows are often considered the most important part of any wedding, and this is generally the most important area in which to solicit the couple's opinions. After all, these are their vows that they are making to one another. This is the literal substance of their marital contract and union together.

Many couples prefer to write their own vows, and you should encourage the couple to do so. Feel free to share examples with them from different faith traditions as a starting point. Make sure you have an extra printed copy of the final result in your folder for the wedding day.

[When you've finished the script, show the couple what you've composed.] Even if you write the entire ceremony by yourself, it's up to the couple to finalize the plan. Some couples might want to be somewhat surprised during the ceremony, but it's always a good idea to have them take a look at your introduction (since it sets the tone) and any statements you might make about the meaning of marriage and their relationship together. If they don't care about being surprised, please have them read the whole thing. Be receptive and accommodate any changes they request (after all, it is their ceremony).

8. Practice the Ceremony

Before the day of the ceremony rehearsal, take time to practice reading through your script. Make notes about where to pause for dramatic effect. Don't talk to fast. Consider re-formatting the document with line breaks to encourage yourself to slow down. Practice saying words that might get stuck on your tongue. Practice them again. Increasing your familiarity with the text is a great way to anchor yourself and have a touchstone in case you somehow get emotional or apprehensive on the big day.

Read through the script in front of a mirror to practice making eye contact. In addition, make sure the couple practice their lines and vows in advance. Practice the ceremony several times so that you feel very comfortable with the full reading. Five years after the ceremony, no one will remember what you said, but they will remember the tone and feeling of the ceremony. If you feel comfortable with the script, then you will communicate better.

When done well, a ceremony renews and refreshes people in an emotional way. So what does this mean for you as a wedding officiant? It means you don't have to offer guests groundbreaking insights into the existential meaning of marriage. You just have to be prepared and be yourself. You were chosen to officiate this wedding for a reason. So be prepared, and be yourself. And be engaging.

You've probably been to enough weddings to know that they can easily turn into a boring and tedious affair. Even if you have a well-written ceremony script laced with loving and inspirational words, you still need to communicate those words in a way that people will most appreciate. Delivery matters. What you say is important, but you should also think about how these words are communicated to everyone.

You are in the best position to deliver a good performance if you are comfortable with both the material and the flow of the script. So practice the script and review the material. Do this several times and you will be prepared. Once you are prepared, you will be unencumbered. You can then focus on your delivery, and you will conduct an excellent wedding ceremony.

9. Deliver the Ceremony

Make sure to get plenty of sleep the night before the ceremony. Everyone else can party, and you can join them after the ceremony. But don't underestimate the importance of being completely rested. You're expected to deliver a moving and thoughtful marriage ceremony, and you can't do this hungover. You will be the center of attention, and you can't afford to make compromises with your overall effectiveness.

Make sure you have your ceremony script on hand, along with a few extra copies in case there are any problems. You will need hard copies printed out so that your delivery is not dependent on technology that could be compromised.

You'll also want to bring along copies of the couple's vows as a backup, as well as any readings that take place during the ceremony. If anyone forgets these critical documents, chances are they're going to look to you for guidance. Stay calm and confident as you guide the ceremony. You were chosen with great care because you are special to the couple.

Please consider this list of non-verbal speaking tips that will help give you a more powerful and dynamic presence from which to deliver the ceremony:

Non-Verbal Tips for Being an Engaging Officiant:

Eye Contact: When you make eye contact with people as you speak, you build a bond with them. Memorize your opening words and deliver them looking at the couple and their guests. This will help make everyone feel more comfortable, as if you'll be "talking to them, not at them." This will increase the overall empathy and responsiveness between everyone. And this will further aid in giving the ceremony a real and authentic feeling.

Smile: It's important that you have a reassuring presence, and the single easiest way to do this is to smile. So smile at people and offer little waves of acknowledgement when appropriate. You're the center of attention. Some people will be envious of you, and some will be glad they're not in your shoes. But regardless of what others feel, you are the person standing in front of everyone, and you will be the person opening, closing, and running through the whole ceremony. So remember to smile.

Smiling communicates across languages and through cultures. Be happy for the couple, and reflect with happiness that of all the people they could have chosen to solemnize their vows – they chose you – so be appreciative and thankful for this opportunity to help them on this very special day. And smile.

Body Orientation: When the couple stands in front of you, make sure they're facing each other so the guests can see their profiles. The same is true with the groomsmen and bridesmaids. You will stand a few feet ahead of the couple, and you'll be positioned to deliver your ceremony between them. If you have any question about where people should stand, please refer to our "Processional, Recessional and Position Assignment Diagram."

Stand straight up, don't hunch. If the microphone is on a stand, adjust it ahead of time to the correct height so you're not leaning down into it. With solid preparation, you won't have to be glued to your script text, so you can stand straight up, look directly at the couple and their guests, and project an excellently delivered ceremony.

Standing and Spacing: Oftentimes couples don't know how exactly to stand or what to do in the ceremony, so make sure they're not standing too far apart (or too close) and remind them to relax and enjoy themselves on this special day. Perhaps you would want to suggest that they hold hands, at least as an initial reference point for how close they want to be to one another.

The three of you will want to stand close enough to the front row of seats so that an intimacy is created. If you are standing in front of an arch, make sure the flowers or other foliage don't droop on you.

Voice & Pacing: Be animated, and avoid speaking in monotone. Don't rush. Pause between sentences to emphasize your message. It is important that you enunciate every word clearly, with some words deserving of extra emphasis. Allowing for pauses gives the guests an opportunity to think about what you've said, which is necessary if they are going to enjoy themselves.

Be conscious that you are basically the tour guide on this small emotional journey that everyone has joined together to produce and witness. There's no hurry, and the most important thing is that your delivery is clear and well-timed so that nothing important is lost. After all, both you and the couple have spent a lot of time preparing the ceremony script, so it is important to do everyone justice and match your great script with a great delivery.

Use controlled and measured breathing to ease any nerves or jitters. Do not wring your hands or pace around if your start to feel apprehensive, as these physical compulsions can feed back into your psychological and physiological maintenance capacities. Stay composed, stay calm, and use controlled and measured breathing to ease your mind should you become apprehensive.

Attire and Composure: Ask the couple their preference for what you will wear. Specifically, how formal should the attire be? Should you prepare for either a full suit or a dress? If you're expected to wear a full suit, what color should the suit, tie, and shirt be? Similarly, if you're expected to wear a dress, how long should it be and what color?

The couple may ask you to just use your own best judgement about what you should wear. In this situation, it is more customary to match officiant colors to the groom. Generally speaking, either a dark colored dress or a dark colored suit with a white shirt are considered to be the best compliments for the groom and his groomsmen. You definitely don't want your clothes to distract from the bride and groom.

Although your title is "minister," what you really are is the "host" of the ceremony. And like the host of a party, you want everyone to enjoy themselves. Please reflect on the parties that you have attended and what makes a good host at these events.

- A good host has good confidence and great composure;
- A good host is charming, generous, high-minded and attentive;
- A good host has great people skills, shows respect to everyone, and has a winning team spirit;
- A good host smiles a lot and lets everyone be themselves (including the host).

Please see that these are most likely the reasons why the couple choose you personally to stand in front of all their family and friends and have *you* to officiate *their* wedding. Because out of everyone they are close to, *you* are the person to best embody all of these dynamic skills and amazing personal attributes listed above. You are the best host that they have. The couple chose you for a reason. They have faith in you for a reason. Take a second to reflect on these facts.

10. Sign the Marriage Certificate

After the conclusion of the wedding, and you are satisfied that the marriage license is valid and all the information is presented correctly, complete the fields relevant to you and sign the license along with any required witnesses. If the marriage license asks for your title, write "Minister."

When you become ordained with North Shore Universal Church, you are accepted into our church as a minister. It is with this title, Minister, that you have the authority to perform marriage, and your "Church Affiliation" will be with us: North Shore Universal Church.

If you're asked whether the proceeding will be "Civil or Religious," you should answer that you will be performing a "Religious" ceremony. If necessary, you can characterize your denominational beliefs as you best determine. Even if you perform a ceremony that is entirely secular in nature, you will be doing so in your capacity as a minister, which is a "Religious" authority. In general, a wedding ceremony is only registered as "Civil" when it has been performed by a public official, a notary public, a judge, a magistrate, or another officer of the court.

Many states require that one or two witnesses also sign the marriage license. The witness/es must complete their required fields on the license and sign the document. Traditionally, this is done by the maid of honor and/or the best man.

Depending on the state, it can be the responsibility of either the couple or the minister to return the completed marriage license. The license must be returned to either the office from which it was issued, or to another approved government office. The license can be returned either in person or through the mail. Specific instructions should be included with the marriage license when the couple does their initial filing.

After the couple's marriage license is returned to the county courthouse, they will make a copy and then file the original with a state-level government office. In most states this is the Bureau of Vital Statistics or Department of Health. The couple should also receive a certified copy of the marriage license within a few weeks of its return.

Once this last step is done, the wedding is official, the couple is legally bound in the contract of a marital union, and everyone is appreciative of the memorable wedding ceremony that you conducted. Your ministry has enriched the world through this small measure of commitment and sacrifice. You have repaid the couple the honor they bestowed upon you. You delivered an excellent ceremony and fulfilled all responsibilities with state and local government. You were a great host. Everyone thanks you.

NSUC Comprehensive Wedding Ceremony Script

Guide to the NSUC Comprehensive Wedding Ceremony Script

Our NSUC Ceremony Script is intended to be comprehensive such that it is amendable and useable in a large variety of situations. It is built to be flexible and interchangeable. Most ceremony chapters have included multiple sections and subsection passages that could be used as substitutes for each other. These sections and subsections are all divided into separate paragraphs, are individually notated within each chapter, and are distinguished with different decimal digits or letters.

For example, in the first chapter, here identified as the "Opening Words" chapter, there are nine different sections: 1.1 through 1.9. Each of these nine different sections are completely interchangeable – you could use any one of them and completely dispose of the rest. Similarly, you could string together multiple sections that you or the couple find particularly poignant.

For example, in the first chapter of the "Opening Words," you could string together sections 1.1 and 1.3. In this scenario, you could read section 1.1, and then follow it up with section 1.3. Similarly, you could read section 1.3 first, and then follow it up with section 1.1. The sectional order within each chapter can be moved around. But the chapters themselves need to stay in the order of their numerical progression.

The idealized wedding structure followed here in this book is listed below. Each chapter should stay in the order listed below:

Wedding Ceremony Chapters

1. Opening Words
2. Query
3. Blessings
4. Readings
5. Introduction to the Vows
6. The Vows
7. Introduction to the Ring Vows
8. The Ring Vows
9. Ring Ceremony Affirmation
10. Unity Ceremony (Candle, Sand, Rose, Water)
11. Signing of the Marriage License
12. Meditation or Prayer
13. Pronouncement
14. Closing Words
15. Speaking to the Children
16. Presentation of the Couple

While it is imperative to maintain the exact numerical/hierarchal order of each chapter of this ceremony, it is ok to dispense with unneeded chapters. For example, you obviously will not include chapter sixteen, "Speaking to the Children" if neither of the couple has any children. Similarly, you will make editing decisions as you compile and customize your idealized script, and in these decisions, you may dispense with most of the comprehensive script outlined below. That is the idea. We intend to give you more than you will need.

North Shore Universal Church

In trimming down the script, please make prudent decisions and consult the couple before dispensing with entire chapters. They may have expectations based on conventions or past experiences that they've witnessed themselves. You would not want them to be disappointed in waiting for a chapter or section that you may have omitted without first consulting them.

Many of the sections are broken down still further, and the lower ordered subsections of the main sections are denoted by letters. For example, chapter three, "The Blessings," has five distinct sections, 3.1 through 3.5. And each of these five sections is divided still further into two additional subsections. So altogether, chapter three has ten separate subsections. It is important to maintain the numerical order when reading though each subsection. For example, subsection 3.1A needs to proceed subsection 3.1B, or neither passage will make much sense.

The subsections cannot be re-ordered hierarchically, nor can they be paired with different subsections. For example, subsection 3.1A and 3.1B must be grouped together, and in that exact order; they cannot be paired with other subsections (ie: 3.1A cannot not be paired with 3.5B).

When writing the couple's ceremony, please keep in mind that no one has enormous expectations for what you will say. The actual words are less important than the overall tone, which is what will ultimately be remembered. Most attendants generally want a pleasant wedding and plan for a relatively short ceremony that will be neither too long or too boring. And while everyone could well appreciate your enthusiasm, a wedding is not the time and place for an officiant to deliver any type of long lecture on "what is marriage."

With the exception of the couple's parents, most wedding attendants' attention span is very limited. The 20-25 minute

Wedding Officiant Manual

mark is ideal for most ceremonies, starting from when the officiant first takes his or her place until the time the couple is being presented as a union. When done well, the wedding ceremony should leave everyone feeling refreshed and happy. After the ceremony, everyone will head off to the reception, excited to celebrate on behalf of the couple, and appreciative of your excellent work.

So write a great script! Make the couple happy and proud of their decision to involve you as their wedding officiant. Because they know you will help put everyone in a great mood by acting as a great host. And because they are confident in your ability to write and delivery a great wedding ceremony. Make sure your script isn't too long, not too short, and make sure to hit all the right parts. We have all the pieces you'll need for your script below. Have a great journey.

North Shore Universal Church

Wedding Script Template

WELCOMING

[the officiant welcomes friends and family and talks about use of cameras]

The procession will begin shortly.

PROCESSION

[wedding party enters]

OPENING WORDS

1.1 Love consists of this, that two solitudes protect and touch and greet one another.

1.2 What greater thing is there for two human souls than to feel that they are joined together to strengthen each other in all labor, to minister to each other in all sorrow, to share with each other in all gladness, and to be one with each other in the silent, unspoken memories?

Opening Poem: "To See the Sun" (E. E. Cummings)

> To see the sun
>
> to reach for the fire
>
> to hear behind all the clamor
>
> the song of life.
>
> There's time for laughing and
>
> there's time for crying,
>
> for hoping, for despair,
>
> for peace, and for longing,
>
> a time for silence,
>
> and a day for singing,
>
> but more than all,
>
> there is a time for timelessness. *(E. E. Cummings)*

~ ~

1.4 Marriage is an institution, ordained by the state, sanctioned by the church, and made honorable by the faithful keeping of good people through the ages. It is, therefore, not to be entered into unadvisedly or lightly, but following due consideration and with reverence. This celebration is the outward symbol of a sacred and inward union of hearts, created by loving purpose and kept by abiding will. Into this estate, Bride/Groom and Bride/Groom come now to be joined.

1.5 Dearly beloved, we are gathered together in the sight of God and in the face of this company to join together Bride/Groom and Bride/Groom in marriage. These two shall make a vow to each other, loving and loved, testifying before us of the blending of their ways and the wedding of their hearts. Before us they shall come together into that estate of marriage which has been treasured and made honorable by faithful keeping, and which, in the presence of God, before whom the secrets of all hearts are disclosed, couples enter reverently, thoughtfully, and in the joy that comes to those who truly love.

1.6 To be true, this outward ceremony must be but a symbol of that which is inner and real - a union of hearts, which religion may bless and the province make legal, but which neither can create. Marriage partakes of the mystery of creation. It grows through the joy of life fully shared, and grows again through pains given and forgiven. While it can be a fount of great happiness, it is not meant for happiness alone, but also for the growth of new qualities of life. Two separate people become more complete because of being together. To this end, there must be a consecration of each to the other, and of both to the noblest purposes of life.

1.7 We have been called together as witnesses to the happiness which this couple has found together, and to the pledges they will make, each to the other, for the mutual service of their common life. We rejoice with them that out of all the world they have found each other, and that they will henceforth find the deeper meaning and richness of human life in sharing it with each other.

1.8 Bride/Groom and Bride/Groom, you have freely decided to commit yourselves to each other in a close and continuing relationship, in which your lives will flow together. In the presence of these witnesses, you will exchange your pledges of that commitment, affirming your intention to strengthen and cherish the relationship you are building together, and to find through the sharing of your lives with each other a unity which will take you out of the loneliness of the isolated self.

❂ 1.9 We are gathered here to join Bride/Groom and Bride/Groom in marriage. It is fitting that you, their families and friends, are here to witness and to participate in their wedding, for the ideals, the understanding, and the mutual respect which they bring to their marriage have their roots in the love, friendship, and guidance you have given them. Marriage makes us aware of the changes wrought by time, but this relationship will continue to draw much of its beauty and meaning from intimate associations with the past.

QUERY

2.1 Bride/Groom and Bride/Groom, have you come here freely and without reservation to give yourselves to each other in marriage in the presence of all here present?

Couple: We have.

2.2 Do you now declare that you have no knowledge of any impediment to your being lawfully joined in matrimony?

2.3 Couple: We do.

BLESSINGS

3.1a (to parents): I now address Bride/Groom's and Bride/Groom's parents. Will you please stand. As our sons and daughters find partners and found the homes of the next generation, each family is enlarged. Do you, who have nurtured these two, give your blessing to their union and their home? If so, please respond, "We do."

3.1b Parents: We do.

Please be seated.

3.2a (to family): I now address Bride/Groom's and Bride/Groom's immediate family/specific relatives such as sisters, brothers, children, ...Will you please stand. As Bride/Groom and Bride/Groom join together in marriage, each family is enlarged. Do you, who have loved these two for all of their lives or all of your lives, give your blessing to their union and their home? If so, please respond, "We do."

3.2b Family: We do.

Please be seated.

3.3a (to family and friends): I now address all of Bride/Groom's and Bride/Groom's family and friends. Please rise. A marriage is, above all, an intimate relationship between two persons. But it also has its wider ramifications into the lives of relatives and friends, and into the community at large. Do you who are here assembled pledge your support to Bride/Groom and Bride/Groom in the commitment that they celebrate today? If so, please respond, "We do."

    3.3b Family and Friends: We do.

    Please be seated.

    3.4a (to family and friends): I now address all of Bride/Groom's and Bride/Groom's family and friends. Please rise. Do you, who have known Bride/Groom and Bride/Groom for many years and have seen them through times of joy and sorrow, now give your blessing to their union? If so, please respond, "We do."

    3.4b Family and Friends: We do.

    Please be seated.

    3.5a (to family and friends): I now address all of Bride/Groom's and Bride/Groom's family and friends. Please rise. As Bride/Groom and Bride/Groom publicly declare their love for one another and the commitment they freely make to one another this day, we can express our support for this union. I ask all of you who are gathered here today, do you who know and care for Bride/Groom and Bride/Groom now give them your blessings as they commit to this relationship? If so, please respond, "We do."

    3.5b Family and Friends: We do.

    Please be seated.

North Shore Universal Church
READINGS

Poem: "How do I Love Thee" (Elizabeth Barrett Brownig)

How do I love thee? Let me count the ways.

I love thee to the depth and breadth and height

My soul can reach when feeling out of sight

For the end of being and ideal grace.

I love thee to the level of every day's

Most quiet need, by sun and candlelight.

I love thee freely, as men strive for right.

I love thee purely, as they turn from praise.

I love thee with the passion put to use

In my old griefs, and with my childhood's faith.

I love thee with a love I seemed to lose

With my lost saints,- I love thee with the breath,

Smiles, tears of all my life!- and if God choose,

I shall but love thee better after death. *(Elizabeth Barrett Browning)*

~ ~

Reading from: **The Prophet** (Khalil Gibran)

Love one another, but make not a bond of love. Let it rather be a moving sea between the shores of your souls. Fill each other's cup, but drink not from one cup. Give one another of your bread, but eat not from the same loaf. Sing and dance together, and be joyous, but let each one of you be alone, even as the strings of a lute are alone, though they quiver with the same music. Give your hearts, but not into each other's keeping, for only the hand of Life can contain your hearts. And stand together, yet not too near together, for the pillars of the temple stand apart, and the oak tree and the cypress grown not in each other's shadow. But let there be spaces in your togetherness, and let the winds of heaven dance between you. Love one another, but make not a bond of love. *(Khalil Gibran)*

~~~~~~~~~~~~~~~~~~~~~~~~~~~

4.1 May your marriage bring you all the deep joy a marriage can bring. And may life also grant you patience, tolerance, and understanding. May you always need one another, not so much to fill your emptiness as to help you know your fullness. May you want one another, but not out of lack. May you entice, but not compel one another. May you embrace, but not encircle one another. May you succeed in all important ways with one another and not fail in the little graces. May you look for things to praise, and often say "I love you." And take no notice of small faults. If you have quarrels that push you apart, may both of you have good sense enough to take the first step back. May you enter into the mystery which is the awareness of one another's presence, physical and spiritual together, warm and near when you are side by side, and warm and near when you are in separate rooms or even in distant cities. May you have happiness, and may you find it in making one another happy. May you have love, and may you find it in loving.

4.2 Awed by the many meanings of this hour and overjoyed by its promises, we hope that the spirit of trust, understanding, and love may be with Bride/Groom and Bride/Groom through all the years that lie ahead. Whatever the trials and testings that may come, may they trust each other wholly, for, without such faith, marriage is a mockery; may they understand each other, for without understanding, there is neither acceptance nor forgiveness; and may they truly love each other, for without love, marriage is an empty shell.

4.3 As they build together a new life and a new home, may that home be bright with the laughter of children and many friends; may it be a haven from the tensions of our time, and a wellspring of strength; and, in all the world, may it be the one place they most want to be.

4.4 So may this shining hour be an open door through which Bride/Groom and Bride/Groom will go forth to build a happy, harmonious marriage. May the years deal gently with them; walking together, may they find far more in life than either would have found alone; and may they come to know their love for one another even more fully.

Reading from: 1ˢᵗ Corinthians: 13; verses 4-13

Love is patient and kind; love is not jealous or boastful; it is not arrogant or rude. Love does not insist on its own way; it is not irritable or resentful; it does not rejoice at wrong, but rejoices in the right. Love bears all things, believes all things, hopes all things, endures all things.

Love never ends. As for prophecies, they will pass away; as for tongues, they will cease; as for knowledge, it will pass away. For our knowledge is imperfect and our prophecy is imperfect; but when the perfect comes, the imperfect will pass away. So faith, hope, love abide, these three; but the greatest of these is love. (Paul the Apostle from First Corinthians)

~ ~

INTRODUCTION TO THE VOWS

5.1 The pledges you will now repeat are a statement of present intent and commitment. They cannot endure unless you make them endure. The spoken word holds no hidden power within itself, for human ingenuity has never yet devised a vow which cannot be broken. We have developed law and conscience, even pride, as keepers of our sacred pledges, but we have also found ways to mitigate each one. So it is not simply to words or to institutions that we appeal at this moment of commitment, but to the resources upon which you can draw from within yourselves.

5.2 Bride/Groom and Bride/Groom, you have carefully considered what you are about to do. In sharing these moments with this group assembled, you are making public what you have felt for quite some time. For this moment of sharing, we thank you, and we extend to you both our hopes and aspirations, our good wishes and our blessings.

5.3 In the quiet of this very special moment, we pause to give thanks for all the rich experiences of life that have brought Bride/Groom and Bride/Groom to this significant point in their lives. We are grateful for the values which have flowed into them from those who have loved them, nurtured them, and pointed them along life's way. We are grateful that within them is the dream of a great love and the resources to use that love in creating a home that will endure. We are grateful for the values which they have found by their own strivings. And now, as they make their promises to each other, may they make them with the deepest insight into their meaning and with their fullest sincerity. May this be but the beginning of a relationship that will grow and mature with each passing year, so that the later days become even more wonderful than the early ones.

VOWS

Please hold hands as you make your vows. Bride/Groom and Bride/Groom, repeat after me:

6.1 In the presence of these witnesses, I take you, Bride/Groom (name), to be my lawful wedded husband/wife/partner, to have and to hold from this day forward, for better, for worse, for richer, for poorer, in sickness or in health, in sorrow or in joy, to love and to cherish, as long as we both shall live.

6.2 Bride/Groom (name), I take you to be my lawful wedded husband/wife/partner, to be the mother/father of my children, to be the companion of my days. We shall bear together whatever of sorrow and adversity life may lay upon us. We shall share together whatever of joy and fulfillment life may hold in store.

6.3 I pledge to you, Bride/Groom (name), a life of giving and of hoping, a life of growing and of loving. I shall dedicate to you both my work and my play. I shall be with you in your tears and in your laughter, just as I shall bring to you my joys and my sorrows. I take you to be my lawful wedded husband/wife/partner and I pledge to you honor, faith, and love.

6.4 From this day forward, Bride/Groom (name), you shall be my lawful wedded husband/wife/partner, together to love, to work and to share, to grow and to understand, to discover a deeper, fuller life.

North Shore Universal Church

6.5 I take you, Bride/Groom (name), to be no other than yourself. Loving what I know of you, trusting what I do not yet know, with respect for your integrity, and faith in your abiding love for me, I accept you as my lawful wedded husband/wife/partner, through all our years, and in all that life may bring us.

6.6 I take you, Bride/Groom (name), to be my lawful wedded husband/wife/partner, to share with me all the wonders life has to offer, through good times and bad, through laughter and tears, as long as we both shall live.

6.7 I commit myself to you, Bride/Groom (name), as your lawful wedded husband/wife/partner, for all the risings and settings of the sun, for all the days of fullness and in barren times, in the foreknowledge of joy and pain, strength and weariness, direction and doubt. I pledge myself to deepening in love as long as time is ours. I take you as my lawful wedded husband/wife/partner.

6.8 I take thee, Bride/Groom (name), to be my lawful wedded husband/wife/partner, to learn and grow with, to come to in both happiness and sorrow, to confide in and trust above all others, to respect you in everything as an equal partner, but, above all, to love you with all my being.

6.9 Bride/Groom, make your vows to Bride/Groom.

[Bride/Groom speaks the vows]

INTRODUCTION TO THE RING VOWS

Please drop hands.

May I please have the rings.

7.1 The circle is the symbol of the sun and the earth and the universe. It is a symbol of holiness and of perfection and peace. In these rings, it is the symbol of unity, in which your two lives are now joined in one unbroken circle, in which, wherever you go, you will always return unto one another to your togetherness.

7.2 The ring symbolizes the unbroken circle of endless love. It is worn on the third finger because of an ancient Greek belief that a vein from that finger is connected directly to the heart, thus symbolizing the depth and sincerity of love.

7.3 May your ring always be the symbol of the unbroken circle of love. Love freely given has no beginning and no end. Love freely given has no giver and no receiver. You are each the giver and each the receiver. May your rings always call to mind the freedom and the power of this love.

7.4 These rings are tokens of the covenant of love you enter into today. We bless them with the elements of earth, air, fire, and water, remembering the sacredness from which our lives and our world are formed. By the power of earth, we consecrate these rings, that they may be a symbol of the unfailing steadfastness of your devotion. (Dip the rings into salt.) Just as the earth is round and supports you, so is love a circle with no beginning and no end and each point interdependent, upholding the whole. May your rings always call to mind the strength of the circle of love.

By the power of air, we consecrate these rings, that they may be a symbol of the communication that fuels the flame of love in your hearts. (Pass the rings through the element of air with feather and incense.) Air is the breath of our lives. It carries the freedom of communication and the power of purification. May the empty centers of your rings call to mind your willingness to speak honestly with one another, and to clearly hear each other with understanding.

By the power of fire, we consecrate these rings, that they may be a symbol of your passion to be with one another. (Pass rings above the candle flame.) Just as one flame lights another and does not grow the less, so may your fires nourish each other. May the brightness of your rings call to mind your ardent desire to learn and create together.

By the power of water, we consecrate these rings, that they may be a symbol of the easy flow and sensitivity of right relationship. (Dip the rings in water.) Just as water shapes all things, may your love shape each of you with emotional integrity and harmony, so that your thirst to be known in love shall be satisfied and yet continue.

7.5 From the words of Black Elk, an Oglala Sioux: Everything the power of the world does is done in a circle. The sky is round, and I have heard that the earth is round like a ball, and so are the stars. The wind, in its greatest power, whirls. Birds make their nests in circles, for theirs is the same religion as ours. The sun comes forth and goes down again in a circle. Even the seasons form a great circle in their changing and always come back again to where they were. Life is a circle, from childhood to childhood, and so it is in everything where power moves.

7.6 They marry each other with a ring, a ring of bright water, whose ripples travel from the heart of the sea. They marry each other with a ring of light, the glitter broadcast on the swift river. They marry each other with the sun's circle, too dazzling to see, traced in the summer sky, with a love that propels the orbit of the moon, and with the boundless circle of the stars. This is a marriage to set tides flowing and command the winds to travel or be at rest.

7.7 [may be omitted or combined with other readings from this section.]

We will now bless Bride/Groom's and Bride/Groom's rings with a warming ceremony in which each of you will hold the rings and bless them. When the rings are passed to you, please warm them in your hands for a few seconds while silently praying and giving your blessing to the couple. Then pass the rings to the person beside you.

[the ushers will take the rings from the officiant, pass them through the family and friends, and return them to the officiant]

RING VOWS

8.1. Bride and Groom, repeat after me as you put Bride/Groom's ring on her/his finger:

8.2a I give you this ring as a symbol of our love and unity.

8.2b With this ring, I marry you and pledge to you my faithful love.

8.2c This ring is a symbol of our union, a token of my faith and love. With this ring, I marry you (or I thee wed).

8.2d Bride and Groom, accept this ring as a token of my love and devotion.

8.3 (said by the officiant after each ring is exchanged) May Bride/Groom who gives it and Bride/Groom who wears this ring, honor in life the pledge for which it stands.

RING CEREMONY AFFIRMATION

9.1 These rings are circles unbroken, just as your love for each other is unbroken and complete. May the love between you grow and strengthen through all the years it would take to travel around your rings and come to their ends.

9.2 In giving and receiving rings, Bride/Groom and Bride/Groom have taken unto themselves symbols of all that this marriage means to them, and in wearing these rings, they are joining those meanings with a public statement that they are married. Each of us knows the values of love and devotion, companionship and trust, honor and caring which come in any intimate relationship. Let us take this time to think on these things and share our hopes for Bride/Groom and Bride/Groom.

9.3 You have given each other these rings as special symbols of what you intend that your love and your marriage will mean to you. As you wear them, may your commitment to that ideal be fulfilled abundantly.

UNITY CEREMONY

Please retrieve your bouquet.

Candle

10.1 (if mothers/parents have not lit family candles) As you each take a candle and together light the unity candle, you are symbolizing the union of your lives. There are two of you, yet there is only one life before you. May this life be blessed and ever richer, because of everything you bring to it as individuals.

10.2 Will the mothers/parents please come to the unity candle table.

I now invite Bride/Groom's and Bride/Groom's mothers/parents to light candles signifying the flame of their love for and pride in their children.

[mothers/parents light the family candles]

May the spirit of this love and pride glow forever brightly in their new life.

10.3 Bride/Groom and Bride/Groom, candles have been lit to signify the love and support of your families. As you together light a candle, you are symbolizing the union of your families and the creation of a new life for you. May this life be blessed and ever richer, because of everything you bring to it as individuals.

[together, the couple lights their unity candle and then individually greet their mothers/parents]

10.4 (with children) We want you to share in the life and love of our family home. (all gather around the candles) In the beginning, there is the light of life, and with it, the hope and promise of love. When each of us is born, we receive the light of life and love Bride/Groom and Bride/Groom will now each light a candle to symbolize their lives and the love they bring to each other.

(Couple lights candles) As we live, our lives give light to others; so it is when we join into families. (the children light candles, or the parents light them for them) And now your hearts are uniting to create new love as a family, with its hope and promise for the future. You are all part of the new light, the new family life which we recognize here today. I invite you to light the candle of unity.

Let the light you have kindled together illuminate your lives and the lives of others through both sunshine and shadow in the days to come.

Sand

10.5 As you stand beside each other, may your love always be as constant as the ocean tide; waves flowing endlessly from the depths of the sea. Just as water is an eternal force of life, so is love. Love is the force that allows us to face fear and uncertainty with courage.

You have sealed your relationship by the giving and receiving of rings. But although you will be sharing one life, never forget that you are two separate people. Cherish and affirm your differences. Love each other. Keep your commitment primary. Together you will laugh and cry, be sick and well, be happy and angry, share and grow. Grow sometimes together, sometimes separately.

To symbolize your union and the importance of the individuals within your marriage, two separate colors of sand will be combined. Each one holds its own unique beauty, strength, and character. Each can stand on its own and be whole, without need of anything else. However, when these two are blended together, they create an entirely new and extraordinarily more intricate entity.

Each grain of sand brings to the mixture a lasting beauty that forever enriches the combination. Please pour the sand into this common container to symbolize the union of your two lives.

[couple pours the sand into the container]

May this be a lasting memory of the vows you have made and of your unity.

Rose

10.6 It is now my privilege to present to you a gift to celebrate your union. In the language of flowers, a rose is a symbol of love. Please exchange your roses. (couple exchanges roses) In this exchange you have given each other a gift as partner to partner, which of course is the gift of love.

And it would be my hope that, wherever you make your home, there be an especially appointed place in it for roses. And that on each succeeding anniversary of this occasion, you celebrate it, at least in part, by each of you bringing to the appointed place a rose, as a restatement of love and as a commitment to the vows you have made this day.

In every union there are occasionally difficult issues which arise. When such times come in your union, either of you will remember and bring to the appointed place a rose. The other will see it, understand it as a statement of love, and accept it, remembering love endures all things.

[couple may bring the roses to place on the register table]

Water

10.7 [pedestal covered in white cloth set to one side, with two identical vessels for water either side of a third receptacle containing a water-soluble capsule of green dye]

As you stand beside each other, may your love always be as constant as the ocean tide; waves flowing endlessly from the depths of the sea. Just as water is an eternal force of life, so is love. Love is the force that allows us to face fear and uncertainty with courage.

You have sealed your relationship by the giving and receiving of rings. But although you will be sharing one life, never forget that you are two separate people. Cherish and affirm your differences. Love each other. Keep your commitment primary. Together you will laugh and cry, be sick and well, be happy and angry, share and grow. Grow sometimes together, sometimes separately

The water Bride/Groom and Bride/Groom are holding represents their individual experiences, values and the love and support they have received from family and friends. However, when these two are combined, they create an entirely new and extraordinarily more intricate entity. Each drop of water brings to the mixture an element of Bride/Groom's and Bride/Groom's lives that forever enriches the combination.

Bride/Groom and Bride/Groom, please pour the water into the common container to symbolize the union of your two lives. The joining of Bride/Groom's and Bride/Groom's lives and experiences has created a new life together, which is stronger and more intricate than before. May this be a lasting memory of the vows you have made and of your unity.

SIGNING OF THE MARRIAGE REGISTER AND LICENSE

11.1 We will now sign the register.

[The marriage register and license must be signed before the officiant can legally pronounce the couple married; you can also do this before the ceremony]

MEDITATION OR PRAYER

12.1 We ask that the holy spirit of love may deepen and enrich the lives of those who leave this place as a newly-married couple. We ask that each may be enabled to see life from the other's point of view, that they may be tolerant and large-minded, sympathetic and kind, considerate of weakness and forgiving of faults. May the relationship which today has been publicly expressed and formalized continue to develop richly in the days to come. Whatever changes time may bring, let what has been said and done here remain as a treasured memory and a guide to life.

12.2 Out of this tangled world, these two souls have joined together, bound with the swift sure bonds of love. Their destinies shall now be woven of one design, and their perils and their joys shall not be known apart. As they increase in mutual understanding, may their joy stand victoriously against the storm of circumstances which beats impartially at all our doors. From the rich encouragement of their affection may they complete the unfinished pattern of their true selves. Even as they have chosen each other from the world's multitudes, so let the days and years, now veiled by time, deepen the joy of that choice, and make it abidingly true.

12.3 Bride/Groom and Bride/Groom, I wish you all happiness; but my wishes cannot give it, nor can it come from outward circumstances. It can only come from yourselves, from the spirit within you. You cannot choose what changes and chances are to befall you in the coming years, but you can choose the spirit with which you will meet them. Let it be the spirit of the noble vows in which you have just made your pledges, each to the other. If you take these vows not as a form, but as a bond of honor which you will keep with unswerving loyalty, then, whatever may come, you will have inward happiness, which no pleasures of themselves can give, no sorrows take away. Then the whole of life which awaits you will be an abiding security to yourselves, and a welcome example to others.

12.4 Bride/Groom and Bride/Groom, may the love which has brought you together continue to grow and enrich your lives, bringing peace and inspiration to each of you and to those who know you. May you meet with courage the problems which arise to challenge you; may you meet with strength the troubles that beset you. May your marriage be one of ever-growing depth, meaning, and development, because of the sympathy, understanding, and love which you give to one another in the life you share.

12.5 We know not what the future may bring into the life of this couple, but we pray that together they may be equal to the needs of their tomorrows. May they have patience in time of strain, strength in time of weakness, courage in time of doubt, and above all, a growing love. And now may the love in your hearts and the greatness of life's possibilities give you joy; the assurances of your families' and friends' good wishes give you peace and strength.

12.6 May the blessing that rests upon all who love rest also upon you and fill you with all spiritual grace. May the bond that unites you ever be strengthened. May you so love and work together in the days that are to come that your lives shall be enriched and ennobled by a true and deepening comradeship of mind and heart.

12.7 God of love, we invoke the gentlest blessing upon all true lovers, and especially upon Bride/Groom and Bride/Groom, who have made their vows of marriage and exchanged rings. Grant to each of them a clear sense of self and of each other, and of the responsibilities to each other and to society. To keep these pledges, may they be filled with grace and understanding. May they be devoted, one to the other. May the happiness which they have brought to these moments never lose its freshness, and may it ripen into fuller flower and deepen, until it mingles with the very roots of their being. May they grow ever closer from this day forward, in work, in play, in hope, in counsel, in laughter and tears. May they, in all the changes and chances of life, be true helpers, one to the other. Hand in hand, heart with heart, may they go forth on their journey in such confidence and trust and affection that no suffering or sorrow or loss can ever blight the joy of their comradeship. Amen.

12.8 We ask for Bride/Groom and Bride/Groom a full life – a life rich in meaning, in purpose, in caring, and in joy. We ask not that they be "happy ever after," although we hope that they will feel happy often. We ask what is perhaps a more realistic goal, though by no means a simple one: that they may continually strive to do and be what their inner voices urge them to attain, not a static contentment with each other and with their world, but an ongoing process of exploring the fullness of their own and each other's personality, of helping and being helped by others, of working for the survival of our endangered planet. But let us not ask for them what we would not ask for ourselves. Let us join with them, let us play with them, and work with them, through many more years of friendship and love.

PRONOUNCEMENT

Please hold hands.

13.1 Bride/Groom and Bride/Groom have chosen one another from the many people of the earth. They have declared their love and purpose before this gathering, and have made their pledges, one to another. Now, by the authority vested in me by the North Shore Universal Church, in the State of (your state), I declare that they are married. Let all others honor them and the threshold of their house. May they find here the good beginning for the spending and fruitfulness of many years.

13.2 Bride/Groom and Bride/Groom have grown in knowledge and love of one another. They have agreed in their desire to go forward in life together, seeking an ever richer, deepening relationship. They have pledged themselves to meet sorrow and joy as one family. We rejoice to recognize their marriage: Now, by the authority vested in me by the North Shore Universal Church, in the State of (your state), now pronounce them duly married.

13.3 Since Bride/Groom and Bride/Groom have joined themselves in marriage and have signified their commitment to each other in the joining of hands and the giving and receiving of rings, I, by the authority vested in me by the North Shore Universal Church, in the State of (your state), now pronounce them husband and bride.

13.4 Bride/Groom and Bride/Groom, in a great sense the two of you were married long before you came here today. Today is merely the sharing of your wishes and hopes with these close friends and relatives who have gathered here this afternoon/evening. We all want you to know that our best wishes are with you at this time. We thank you for sharing this very personal moment with us. Now, by the authority vested in me by the North Shore Universal Church, in the State of (your state), I pronounce you husband and wife.

Please seal your vows with a kiss.

Please take back your bouquet.

CLOSING WORDS

14.1 Now you will feel no rain, for each of you will be shelter to the other.

Now you will feel no cold, for each of you will be warmth to the other.

Now there is no loneliness for you. Now there is no more loneliness.

Now you are two bodies, but there is only one life before you.

Go now to your dwelling place, to enter into the days of your togetherness, and may your days be good and long upon the earth.

14.2 Let us now, in a moment of silence, give our individual blessings to Bride/Groom and Bride/Groom, now married. May the blessing of each of us be felt by you. And may you also sense the blessing which is not ours to give, but which comes from the very heart of life and is known to those who seek it. Go now to walk the ways of the world together, and may your days be good and long upon the earth.

14.3 Go now to walk the ways of the world together. You, (names of children), you, too, have entered this circle of love, where you will be sheltered and warmed until you are grown and go to find your own world. May the days of all of you be good and long upon the earth.

14.4 May all that is noble, lovely, and true abide with you forever. Go now in peace, and may peace attend you all your days.

14.5 Now and forever, may both of you be united in love and harmony. May both of you share your moods and dreams with loving care.

May both of you keep trust in each other, constant and deep.

May you find joy in life, and warm contentment in your marriage.

14.6 May the love in your hearts give you joy. May the greatness of life bring you peace. And may your days be good and your lives be long upon the earth.

14.7 We are happy to be sharing in the rejoicing of this hour. May all who love Bride/Groom and Bride/Groom continue to rejoice in the commitments they have made to one another. We ask for them that the meaning of these moments may abide throughout their lives, and that in pleasant ways or in the midst of trials, they may be a comfort and a joy to each other. May each bring intelligence and commitment as well as faith to the task this is set before them. May they maintain enduring respect and trust. May their home be a place of peace for them and all who enter it. May all who follow their lives with interest and affection have cause often to rejoice, not only in their happiness, but also in their brave and generous living. Amen.

14.8 And now may the glory which rests on all who love rest upon you and bless you and keep you. May it fill you with happiness and a gracious spirit. And despite all changes of time and fortune, may all that is noble and lovely and true abound in your hearts and abide with you and give you strength in your days together.

SPEAKING TO THE CHILDREN

15.1 (speaking to children) Bride/Groom are very excited/happy today. I hope you are excited/happy, too. You know how much they love you. They are starting life together today in a new way. This does not mean that your father/mother is less important or doesn't count. But it does mean that Bride/Groom and Bride/Groom are creating a home for you where you will always be welcome. It is a place where you can share your feelings and your dreams and your wishes. Bride/Groom and Bride/Groom love each of you. They want to be as open with their thoughts and feelings as you are.

Each of you brings a special warmth to this family that is just yours. For your part in making this family, Bride/Groom and Bride/Groom are deeply thankful, and they love you very much.

15.2 (children's names) Do you share the hopes of Bride/Groom and Bride/Groom, and wish them happiness in the years to come?

15.3 Bride/Groom and Bride/Groom, you bring a child (children) to this marriage? You are making a new family. Do you affirm that your child (children) are a sacred responsibility, and do you welcome them to this new family with love?

PRESENTATION

Please link arms and turn to face your family and friends.

16.1 It is my honor and joy to present _____!

16.2 Friends, it is an honor and my joy to present to you the newly married couple/spouses/husband and wife, _____!

16.3 (ask for the children to come or be brought forward to join the couple) Friends, it is my joy to present _____ and (names of children).

[wedding party leaves]

Supplemental Readings

Wedding Prayer by Robert Louis Stevenson

Lord, behold our family here assembled.

We thank you for this place in which we dwell,

for the love that unites us,

for the peace accorded us this day,

for the hope with which we expect the morrow,

for the health, the work, the food,

and the bright skies that make our lives delightful;

for our friends in all parts of the earth.

Amen. *(Robert Louis Stevenson)*

~~~~~~~~~~~~~~~~~~~~~~~~~~

Wedding Blessing by his holiness the 14th Dalai Lama

Take into account that great love and great achievements involve great risk.

And that a loving atmosphere in your home

is the foundation for your life.

Be gentle with the earth,

be gentle with one another.

When disagreements come

remember always to protect the spirit of your union.

When you realize you've made a mistake,

take immediate steps to correct it.

Remember that the best relationship is one

in which your love for each other

exceeds your need for each other.

So love yourselves, love one another,

love all that is your life together

and all else will follow.

~~~~~~~~~~~~~~~~~~~~~~~~~~~

"Blessing of the Hands" by Unknown

These are the hands of your partner, young and strong and full of love, holding your hands as you promise to love each other today, tomorrow, and forever. These are the hands that will work alongside yours as together you build your future. These are the hands that will hold you and comfort you in grief and uncertainty. These are the hands that will countless times wipe the tears from your eyes, tears of sorrow and joy. These are the hands that will hold your family as one. These are the hands that will give you strength. And these are the hands that even when wrinkled and aged, will still be reaching for yours, still giving you the same unspoken tenderness with just a touch.

~~~~~~~~~~~~~~~~~~~~~~~~~~

"What is Love" by Unknown

Sooner or later we begin to understand that love is more than verses on valentines and romance in the movies. We begin to know that love is here and now, real and true, the most important thing in our lives. For love is the creator of our favorite memories and the foundation of our fondest dreams. Love is a promise that is always kept, a fortune that can never be spent, a seed that can flourish in even the most unlikely of places. And this radiance that never fades, this mysterious and magical joy, is the greatest treasure of all – one known only by those who love.

~~~~~~~~~~~~~~~~~~~~~~~~~~

Apache Wedding Blessing

Now you will feel no rain, for each of you will be shelter for the other. Now you will feel no cold, for each of you will be warmth to the other. Now there will be no loneliness, for each of you will be companion to the other. Now you are two persons, but there is only one life before you. May beauty surround you both in the journey ahead and through all the years, may happiness be your companion and your days together be good and long upon the earth. Treat yourselves and each other with respect, and remind yourselves often of what brought you together. Give the highest priority to the tenderness, gentleness and kindness that your connection deserves. When frustration, difficult and fear assail your relationship – as they threaten all relationships at one time or another – remember to focus on what is right between you, not only the part which seems wrong. In this way, you can ride out the storms when clouds hide the face of the sun in your lives – remembering that even if you lose sight of it for a moment, the sun is still there. And if each of you takes responsibility for the quality of your life together, it will be marked by abundance and delight.

~~~~~~~~~~~~~~~~~~~~~~~~~~~

Wedding Rehearsal and Processional Primer

As the wedding day approaches, make sure you have plenty of time set aside for the rehearsal of the ceremony, including a rehearsal that involves yourself and the entire wedding party. This is your best opportunity to work out any lingering confusions or unanticipated complications that may have arisen as you seek to ground the ceremony in the days before it is conducted. The wedding rehearsal will include the entire wedding party, including all groomsmen, bridesmaids, ring bearers, and flower girls. At the rehearsal, you will run through all major footwork and physical positioning within the designated ceremony space so that everyone will know where to stand, where to walk to, and how much spacing they should have between themselves. If no one else in the wedding party takes charge in this situation, consider doing it yourself provided that you can do so in a way that most everyone would appreciate. The important thing is to move through the rehearsal in a manner that is both timely and comprehensive. Everyone needs to know what they need to know, and the sooner the better.

At the rehearsal, you are not practicing the ceremony itself – you are only practicing walking in and walking out, and making sure everyone knows where to stand. Since the officiant is one of the first people to enter at the beginning of the ceremony, it's not possible for the officiant to "cue" each group and tell them when to start walking. This is normally the responsibility of the coordinator at your ceremony site, or your wedding planner if you have one. Many of our couples will also ask a friend or family member to help run the rehearsal and cue everyone for their entrance to the ceremony, which is a great option. Ideally, you want the same person who is running the rehearsal to be in charge of the ceremony on your wedding day as well – that continuity will really help ensure that there isn't any confusion on the wedding day.

The wedding rehearsal should be a quick, easy, and straightforward process. If the ceremony venue doesn't provide a coordinator, you should choose a friend or family member to help everyone along. The best person for this job is, quite frankly, someone who is a little bossy. They will need to be assertive enough to get the whole group to pay attention, but not be so overbearing that it's off-putting to any sensitive families and wedding party. Teachers are almost always the perfect choice for this because they are used to corralling large groups of unruly children. Give them this guide before you arrive, and also give them a copy of your ceremony draft that you have finalized with the couple. They'll have all the information they need to run the rehearsal quickly and efficiently.

North Shore Universal Church

Running the Rehearsal and Practicing the Processional

Follow these easy steps to rehearse the wedding ceremony quickly and easily.

1. **Introduce yourself to the group.** This may sound silly, but it is easy to forget how important this first introduction to everyone is. Let the wedding party know who you are and that you will be leading them through the rehearsal. Kindly ask for everyone's attention to achieve group efficiency and expediency. Your goal is to get through everything quickly so your group can be on its way to rehearsal dinner and celebrate their time together. So you want to ensure that people are paying attention and remain on-task.

2. **Start in the middle.** Instead of starting with the processional (entrance), start by getting everyone into place where they will be standing during the ceremony. Remember that you are practicing walking in and out, so knowing where to stand is the first step. See the diagram below for the standard positions for the couple, officiant, parents, and attendants. It's important to have the wedding party evenly spaced and standing at a slight angle in relation to the wedding guests, with the attendants at each end a little more forward than the Maid of Honor and Best Man. This looks better for pictures, and helps the guests see each person in the wedding party better. Bridesmaids should hold their bouquets in front of them with both hands, and groomsmen should decide on clasping their hands in the front or the back of their body. It's important that everyone do the same thing, especially in the photos. If

everyone is doing something different it tends to look less than ideal in the wedding photos.

3. **Hit the main parts.** Take a look at the ceremony draft and read through the headings aloud, so everyone knows roughly the order of the ceremony. Don't read through the entire ceremony word-for-word or say the vows, save that excitement for the big day. Make a note of any wedding ceremony readings, candle lighting, water, rose, or sand ceremonies, and when the rings will need to be presented. Double check that any items needed during the ceremony like candles or a table will be there that day. No matter what, make sure that everyone (including the couple) knows that they shouldn't stand with their backs to the wedding guests at any point in the ceremony. Even if people need to move around during the ceremony, for example to do a candle lighting ceremony, make sure that they always end up standing in a position where they still face the guests (and the photographer). The last item on the list will be the kiss and, if the couple has chosen to do so, the presentation of the couple.

4. **Practice the processional in reverse first (ie: the recessional).** Since you already have everyone in standing in place, practice the recessional as if the ceremony has just ended and you are all walking out. Start with the kiss and/or the presentation of the couple, and exit in the proper order. The Bride will take her bouquet from the Maid of Honor and exit with the Groom. Typically, the wedding party will exit in pairs even if they enter separately, followed by the Flower Girl and Ring Bearer, and then the parents and grandparents. It's important to make sure that each couple that exits the ceremony leaves enough room between themselves and the couple in front of them. To do this, everyone should agree on a set distance they will wait before walking. Most people choose to start

walking when the couple in front of them is halfway back up the aisle. In general, it's best to leave at least 20 feet between each couple for the sake of pictures, but not much more than that.

Once everyone has successfully exited the ceremony, it's finally time to practice walking back in. If necessary, reorder the groupings/couplings of people into this order:

1) Officiant, Important guests, Grandparents
2) Groom, (and possibly), Best Man, Groomsmen*
3) Parents
4) Bridesmaid, (and possibly) Groomsmen (repeat for as many times as necessary) *
5) Maid of Honor, (and possibly) Best Man*
6) Ringbearers
7) Flower Girls
8) Bride, Father of the Bride

* Many ceremonies do not pair the bridesmaids with the groomsman during the actual processional. These pairings can be exclusive to the recessional.

5. **Begin practicing the processional**. Now that everyone knows where to stand when they enter the ceremony, practicing the entrance should be easy. Line everyone up in the order they will enter. The Officiant, Groom, Best Man, and Groomsmen enter first, typically from the side of the ceremony site but sometimes up the aisle depending on preference. Following them are the grandparents, the parents of the Groom, and the Mother of the Bride. Finally, the Bridesmaids, Maid of Honor, Ring bearers, and Flower Girl enter. While the Officiant, Groom, and Groomsmen normally enter together as a group in a straight line, everyone else needs to be spaced evenly. As with the recessional, it's important to agree upon how much space to

leave between people entering the ceremony – normally about 20-30 feet. The Bride and her escort (typically the Father of the Bride) should not enter until the entire wedding party has entered and is in place. Normally there is a separate piece of music for the Bride's processional, and the officiant will usually say "If everyone will please rise," in order to invite the guests to stand.

6. **Handing off the Bride.** The last item to practice is what happens when the Bride and her escort make it to the front of the ceremony and are standing in front of the Officiant and the Groom. If the escort is a parent of the Bride, they should give her a kiss and congratulate her. The escort then typically shakes the Groom's hand, the Bride hands her bouquet to the Maid of Honor and steps forward next to the groom, and the escort moves to where they will be seated. The Bride and Groom should then be standing facing one another, holding hands in front of the Officiant. At this point, the Maid of Honor can hand off both sets of flowers to one of the Bridesmaids and fix the Bride's train, if necessary.

7. **Do it again.** Now that everyone is in place, practice walking back out and back in one more time to make sure everyone knows what to do. It is obviously best spending a few extra minutes at the rehearsal to make sure that everything goes smooth. Generally speaking, the rehearsal should last about 20 - 30 minutes depending on the level of complexity and number of people involved.

Following the steps above will ensure that everyone knows exactly what to do and where to stand on the wedding day, and that you aren't wasting a lot of time practicing unnecessary parts of the ceremony itself.

North Shore Universal Church

Below is a helpful diagram of where everyone should be standing:

Processional, Recessional, & Position Assignment Diagram

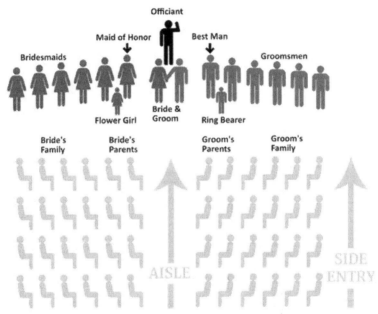

ENTRANCE ORDER
(PROCESSIONAL)

1. Grandparents of the Groom
2. Grandparents of the Bride
3. Officiant, Groom, BestMan, Groomsmen
   (from side entry if desired)
4. Parents of the Groom
5. Mother of the Bride
6. Bridesmaids
7. Maid of Honor
8. Flower Girl and Ring Bearer
9. Bride / Father of the Bride

EXIT ORDER
(RECESSIONAL)

1. Bride and Groom
2. Maid of Honor and BestMan
3. Bridesmaids and Groomsmen
   (in pairs when exiting)
4. Flower Girl and Ring Bearer
5. Parents of the Bride
6. Parents of the Groom
7. Grandparents of the Bride
8. Grandparents of the Groom
9. Officiant
9. Weeding Guests

Variations in Wedding Processions

Many couples choose to forego the traditional wedding ceremony order and some manner of customization, including cultural, religious, or regional variations in their ceremony. Our NSUC Comprehensive Wedding Script wedding can help create a fully customized ceremony for each couple. In addition to the multitude of customizable options and passages within our Script, there are also significant variations of a "standard" ceremony. Some notable variations in ceremonies and processionals are listed here below:

- **LGBTQ+ Ceremonies** – We've found that the only rule for gay weddings is that there are no rules. LGBTQ+ couples can sometimes break the mold entirely, creating a custom ceremony that reflects their relationship while still incorporating a few elements seen at most wedding ceremonies. The order for the processional and recessional may be completely different than the diagram we've provided, sometimes with the wedding party and couple entering together, or having no wedding party at all. We encourage all of our LGBTQ+ friends, colleagues, and affiliated ministers to be creative and work with the couple to create something truly unique and defined by them.

- **The Midwest Processional** – Couples from the Midwest are sometimes surprised to see the Bridesmaids and Groomsmen entering the wedding ceremony separately. Regional differences in wedding traditions are pretty common. In the "Midwest Processional," the Maid of Honor, Best Man, and all of the Bridesmaids and Groomsmen enter the ceremony in pairs. The Officiant and the Groom still enter first from the side, and then the rest of the wedding party enters in reverse order, with the Maid of Honor and Best Man the last to enter before the Flower Girl and Ring Bearer.

- **Multi-Parent Escort** – Many couples choose to be escorted into the ceremony by multiple parents, instead of just by one. While the Father of the Bride traditionally escorts the Bride down the aisle, sometimes couples will want to have their mother and father, or father and step-father, (or whoever) walk them down the aisle together. This isn't just limited to the Bride; there are also plenty of weddings where the Groom is also escorted into the ceremony by his parents. This is often seen in many Jewish and interfaith weddings as well.

- **Jewish Traditional Entrance** – For Jewish and half-Jewish weddings, couples sometimes opt for a traditional Jewish entrance to the wedding ceremony. In this variation, the Officiant enters first, followed by the Groom who is escorted by his parents. When the Groom and his parents reach the wedding canopy, or Chuppah, the Groom stands in the "standard" position but his parents stand under the Chuppah on the opposite side (ie: behind the Officiant's right shoulder, across from the Groom so they can see him). Next, the Bride enters, escorted by her parents, and they take the opposite positions, behind the Officiant's left shoulder. Both sets of parents remain standing at the Chuppah for the entire ceremony.

Breaking with Tradition (but keeping the rehearsal dinner)

Generally speaking, there is no "right" way to do a wedding rehearsal, processional or ceremony, and we encourage officiants and couples to work together to create something that is a unique expression of the couple's love. Traditions are wonderful, and many couples choose to have a traditional rehearsal and procession – others choose to break with tradition and do something entirely different. We encourage you to listen to the couple and do what feels right for them throughout the entire process, whatever that may be.

However, one tradition that is almost always advisable, and that almost everyone generally loves, is the rehearsal dinner. It is definitely the couple's or their planner's responsibility to put together the rehearsal dinner, as there are a lot of loose ends beyond the scoop of the officiant's duties. But you're still expected to show up, enjoy yourself, and get to know everyone so that you can perform your officiant obligations with a greater degree of familiarity and warmth. The rehearsal dinner is always a lot of fun for everyone, and it's a great opportunity to meet some of the people you'll be working with on the big day. So move through the rehearsal swiftly so you can all can get to the after party and enjoy yourselves – there's a wedding going on.

North Shore Universal Church

~ *Notes* ~

North Shore Universal Church

Resources for Emotional and Psychological Support

As members and ministers of North Shore Universal Church, we all rely on each other to uphold the values of our organization. This includes being available to give emotional and psychological support to those in need whenever appropriate. As you may understand, some people can and will reach out to church ministers for guidance. This could include the couple being married, or it could include anyone else. Weddings can bring out a lot of emotions and memories for a lot of people, so be conscious that people may reach out. You are, after all, the presiding minister.

A vitally important part of the NSUC mission is our emphasis on encouragement and positivity. A healthy, stable, and positive outlook is key to a well-managed life. Maintaining this mental focus is critical as we navigate the highs and lows of our respective paths. As members and ministers of NSUC, we depend on each other to provide the best light and reflection that we can bring to this world and our community. We all want to be the best person we can be for each other.

If anyone reaches out to you, please consider embracing them to your best capacity and share with them our church ministerial approach to overcoming difficulty in life. Below, we have prepared a brief reading that you can share with anyone who might reach out to you. Please feel free to deliver these thoughts on overcoming significant loss, pain, or other mental anguish as you see fit.

Readings for Emotional and Psychological Encouragement

If your life circumstances change suddenly, and your sense of security and normalcy is disrupted. Stay calm, remain steadfast, and know that you will carry forward. Slow down and do what you can to reinforce your stability. Avoid alcohol and drugs as none of this will help you. And please avoid adopting nervous mannerisms (like a restless leg or wringing your hands), as this will feed back into your own psychology and can aggravate anxiety. It is important to stabilize your perspective and regulate your emotions and energy. Maybe go for a walk or call a friend or family-member, and remember, your perspective matters a lot more than your circumstances.

However, if your circumstances do trouble you, understand that you are not merely the manager of these random circumstances that befall you. Your circumstances will always change, but your perspective on life can be the rock of stability to help you endure difficult periods. Always remember: you create life and have brought into this world amazing evidence of your talents. People love you. And no matter what: *there is always more greatness for you to create*. Indeed, oftentimes it is the people who have progressed the most through time and life who have the most to offer the friends and family in their lives. Remember what you have to offer others in service.

When you hit a serious obstacle in life, and you need to make some important decisions, take it slow and easy. Don't be hard on yourself; forgive yourself any indiscretions that contribute to the situation. Blame or anger will not help you move forward. Look for the good. Be positive and be grateful for this opportunity to improve yourself. Motivational coach Tony Robbins has identified a three-part criterion that can be used in pursuit of making our best decisions at these difficult moments.

1. What are you going to focus on?
2. What does something mean?
3. What are you going to do?

What are you going to focus on? This is critical because focus is the key that unlocks the door whereupon we can confront our obstacles and chart a new and better path. Mental focus can actually determine our emotional feelings, psychology, and physiology. Reflections on anything negative will start to sink your spirits. If you want to feel positive, then you need to focus on the positive things you've known in life.

Focus on the depth of love given to you from all of the people in your life, especially your family and other main players. These people have brought you love because they could see how worthy of this love you have always been. Focus on how this love makes you feel physically. Notice the warmth you feel and the smile on your face when you think of the people who love you. Be grateful.

A healthy outlook is a choice. Choose to be grateful. Studies have shown that gratitude improves self-esteem, enhances relationships, improves quality of sleep, and expands longevity. Gratitude is good medicine in difficult times, so make this choice. Again and again, make the choice to be grateful. If you become worried or fearful, recognize this and *choose to pull your mind back into a state gratefulness.* Make this choice every time, the same way you might keep a distracted puppy from going off track, with patience and good humor. Always come back to being grateful and reflect on the love you've known.

What does something mean? Context brings clarity, and clarity enables power. Don't feed and enlarge your troubles by misunderstanding the contexts within which they occur. By hyper-fixating on our troubles, we can paralyze the very action we need to move past them. And while it is clearly necessary to "keep it all in perspective," this can be a difficult thing to do during life's downturns – if only because of emotional paralyzation and psychological disarray.

So call a friend or family member and have a verbal conversation. They will remind you of how far you've come and your personal fortitude that got you there. Keep everything in context. Loss happens inevitably in life. A lot of people lose important relationships, positions, money or other resources. Everyone loses friends and/or family. But we owe it to each other, especially our loved ones who have invested their time in us, to really keep all of life's challenges – and miracles – in their full and proper context so we can move forward.

If no loved one is available to speak with you, then you need to focus on calming your mind by yourself. Racing thoughts will not help you, nor will despair or anger. You must actively set all of this aside. If necessary, speak positively to yourself aloud into a mirror, over and over again, hitting inflection points to really *convince* yourself of what you need to know at this time. Within your reassurance, count your blessings and remind yourself of your gratitude. Engage yourself with this positive focus and don't allow racing thoughts to trouble your mind to exhaustion. Remind yourself that everything will work out for the best, including any lessons for you to learn.

What are you going to do? Set goals that motivate you, that are self-rewarding, that make you happy somehow. Know what you want, know why you want it, and know what it takes to get there. Really spend some time exploring all of this. Talk this through with others and/or yourself (ie: break out the mirror again). If necessary, break big goals down into smaller, more specific goals. Keep your focus daily and hourly, writing things down if necessary. Stay busy and keep moving forward. Maintain gratefulness for all of the important things in your life.

Pay attention to what you're getting on this new road and be sensitive to what is working (as well as what's not working). If necessary, change your approach. Refine and change again if necessary. Continue to chart and re-chart your recovery. Communicate regularly with your friends and family, as your concern to be accountable will keep you on course. And Don't Give Up! Failure, loss, and obstacles are all part of life. But you will overcome everything in your time.

~~~~~~~~~~~~~~~~~~~~~~~~~~

Encouraging Scriptures

Facing Danger, Persevere.

Then there is no blame.

Do not complain about this truth.

Enjoy whatever fortune you possess.

   – Chinese Proverb

~ ~

God tells his children, his chosen ones, not to be afraid, because he is with them.

Floods will not overwhelm them and fires will not consume them.

He will bring his sons and daughters from afar and they will be redeemed.

Although their transgressions have burdened him, he will blot those out for his own sake.

They are not to remember these former things for he is doing something new!

He has called them each by name.

They are precious in his eyes and he loves them!

   – Book of Isiah 43; 1-2, 4, 7, 18-19, 24-25

~ ~

Helpful Aphorisms

Have a mind open to everything and attached to nothing.

No one knows enough to be a pessimist.

Humility is the door to restoration.

Get blame out of your life.

There are no justified resentments.

Wisdom is avoiding all thoughts that weaken you.

Trade your expectations for appreciations.

Relax your certainties and embrace bewilderment.

Always remember gratefulness. Gratitude turns what you have into enough.

Gratitude is not only the greatest of virtues but the parent of all others.

Gratitude is the path to the best actualization of life.

Gratitude is the foundation of a God-realized life. A genuinely grateful person has multiple virtues that resound from this core identity. The four virtues on this best path for god-realized living are:

1. Reverence
2. Honesty
3. Kindness
4. Supportiveness

Four Rules for Living, *by Dr. Wayne Dyer*[2]

Some 2,500 years ago, Lao-tzu spoke of "the four cardinal virtues" and noted that when we practice them as a way of life, we come to know and access the truth of the universe. These four virtues don't represent external dogma, but a part of our original nature—by practicing them, we realign with Source and access the powers that Source energy has to offer. According to the teachings of Lao-tzu, the four cardinal virtues represent the surest way to leave habits and excuses behind and reconnect to your original nature. The more your life is harmonized with the four virtues, the less you're controlled by the uncompromising ego.

---

[2] (reprinted from: www.healyourlife.com/four-rules-for-living)

The First Cardinal Virtue: Reverence for All Life

The first cardinal virtue manifests in your daily life as unconditional love and respect for all beings in creation. This includes making a conscious effort to love and respect yourself, as well as to remove all judgments and criticisms. Understand that you are a piece of God, and since you must be like what you came from, you are lovable, worthy, and Godlike. Affirm this as often as you can, for when you see yourself in a loving way, you have nothing but love to extend outward. And the more you love others, the less you need old excuse patterns, particularly those relating to blame.

The Second Cardinal Virtue: Natural Sincerity

This virtue manifests itself as honesty, simplicity, and faithfulness; and it's summed up by the popular reminder to be true to yourself. Using an excuse to explain why your life isn't working at the level you prefer isn't being true to yourself—when you're completely honest and sincere, excuses don't even enter into the picture. The second virtue involves living a life that reflects choices that come from respect and affection for your own nature. Make truth your most important attribute. Walk your talk; that is, become sincere and honest in all that you say and do. If you find this to be a challenge, take a moment to affirm: *I no longer need to be insincere or dishonest. This is who I am, and this is how I feel.* When you know and trust yourself, you also know and trust the Divinity that created you. If you live from honesty, sincerity, and faithfulness to the callings of your spirit, you'll never have occasion to use excuses.

The Third Cardinal Virtue: Gentleness

This virtue personifies one of my favorite and most frequently employed maxims: "When you have the choice to be right or to be kind, always pick kind." So many of your old thinking habits and their attendant excuses come out of a need to make yourself right and others wrong. When you practice this third virtue, you eliminate conflicts that result in your need to explain why you're right. This virtue manifests as kindness, consideration for others, and sensitivity to spiritual truth.

Gentleness generally implies that you no longer have a strong ego-inspired desire to dominate or control others, which allows you to move into a rhythm with the universe. You cooperate with it, much like a surfer who rides with the waves instead of trying to overpower them. Gentleness means accepting life and people as they are, rather than insisting that they be as you are. As you practice living this way, blame disappears and you enjoy a peaceful world.

The Fourth Cardinal Virtue: Supportiveness

This virtue manifests in your life as service to others without any expectation of reward. Once again, when you extend yourself in a spirit of giving, helping, or loving, you act as God acts. As you consider the many excuses that have dominated your life, look carefully at them – you'll see that they're all focused on the ego: *I can't do this. I'm too busy or too scared. I'm unworthy. No one will help me. I'm too old. I'm too tired.* Now imagine shifting your attention off of yourself and asking the universal mind How may I serve? When you do so, the message you're sending is: I'm not thinking about myself and what I can or can't have. Your attention is on making someone else feel better.

The greatest joy comes from giving and serving, so replace your habit of focusing exclusively on yourself and what's in it for you. When you make the shift to supporting others in your life, without expecting anything in return, you'll think less about what you want and find comfort and joy in the act of giving and serving.

The four cardinal virtues are a road map to the simple truth of the universe. To revere all of life, to live with natural sincerity, to practice gentleness, and to be in service to others is to replicate the energy field from which you originated.

~~~~~~~~~~~~~~~~~~~~~~~~~

Ten Stress Management Techniques, by Dr. Wayne Dyer,[3]

There's nothing natural about living a life filled with stress and anxiety, having feelings of despair and depression, and needing pills to tranquilize yourself. Agitated thoughts that produce high blood pressure, a nervous stomach, persistent feelings of discomfort, an inability to relax or sleep, and frequent displays of displeasure and outrage are violating your natural state. Believe it or not, you have the power to create the naturally stress-free and tranquil life you desire. You can utilize this power to attract frustration or joy, anxiety or peace.

Step 1: Remember that your natural state is joy.

You are a product of joy and love; it's natural for you to experience these feelings. You've come to believe that feeling bad, anxious, or even depressed is natural, particularly when people and events around you are in low-energy modes. Remind yourself as frequently as necessary: I come from peace and joy. I must stay in harmony with that from which I came in order to fulfill my dreams and desires. I choose to stay in my natural state. Anytime I'm anxious, stressed out, depressed, or fearful, I've abandoned my natural state.

---

[3] reprinted from: www.healyourlife.com/10-stress-management-strategies-from-wayne-dyer

Step 2: Your thoughts, not the world, cause your stress.

Your thoughts activate stressful reactions in your body. Stressful thoughts create resistance to the joy, happiness, and abundance that you desire to create in your life. These thoughts include: I can't, I'm too overworked, I worry, I'm afraid, I'm unworthy, It will never happen, I'm not smart enough, I'm too old (young), and so on. These thoughts are like a program to resist being tranquil and stress free, and they keep you from manifesting your desires.

Step 3: You can change your thoughts of stress in any given moment, and eliminate the anxiety for the next few moments, or even hours and days.

By making a conscious decision to distract yourself from worry, you've inaugurated the process of stress reduction, while simultaneously reconnecting to the field of all creating intention. It's from this place of peace and tranquility that you become a co-creator with God. You can't be connected to your Source and be stressed at the same time this – this is mutually exclusive. Your Source doesn't create from a position of anxiety, nor does it need to swallow antidepressants. You've left behind your capacity to manifest your desires when you don't choose in the moment to eliminate a stressful thought.

Step 4: Monitor your stressful thoughts by checking on your emotional state right in the moment.

Ask yourself the key question: Do I feel good right now? If the answer is no, then repeat those five magic words: I want to feel good, then shift to: I intend to feel good. Monitor your emotions, and detect how much stress – and anxiety producing thinking you're engaging in. This monitoring process keeps you apprised of whether you're on the path of least resistance or going in the other direction.

Step 5: Make a conscious choice to select a thought that will activate good feelings.

I urge you to choose your thought based exclusively on how it makes you feel, rather than on how popular it is or how well advertised. Ask yourself: Does this new thought make me feel good? No? Well, how about this thought? Not really? Here's another. Ultimately, you'll come up with one that you agree makes you feel good, if only temporarily. Your choice might be the thought of a beautiful sunset, the expression on the face of someone you love, or a thrilling experience. It's only important that it resonate within you emotionally and physically as a good feeling. In the moment of experiencing an anxious or stressful thought, change to the thought you chose, which makes you feel good. Plug it in. Think it and feel it in your body if you can. This new thought that makes you feel good will be of appreciation rather than depreciation. It will be of love, beauty, and receptivity to happiness.

Step 6: Spend some time observing babies, and vow to emulate their joy.

You didn't come forth into this world to suffer, to be anxious, fearful, stressful, or depressed. You came from the God-consciousness of joy. Just watch little babies. They've done nothing to be so happy about. They don't work; they poop in their pants; and they have no goals other than to expand, grow, and explore this amazing world. They love everyone, they're completely entertained by a plastic bottle or goofy faces, and they're in a constant state of love—yet they have no teeth, no hair, and they're pudgy and flatulent. How could they possibly be so joyful and easily pleased? Because they're still in harmony with the Source that intended them here; they have no resistance to being joyful. Be like that baby you once were in terms of being joyful. You don't need a reason to be happy . . . your desire to be so is sufficient.

Step 7: Keep "Rule Number 6" in mind.

This means to suspend the demands of your ego, which keep you separated from intention. When you have a choice to be right or to be kind, pick kind, and push the ego's demand out of the way. Kindness is what you emanated from, and by practicing it, rather than being right, you eliminate the possibility of stress in your moment of kindness. When you find yourself being impatient with anyone, simply say to yourself: "Rule Number 6," and you'll immediately laugh at the piddly little ego that wants you to be first, faster, number one, and to be treated better than the other guy.

Step 8: Accept the guidance of your Source of intention.

You will only come to know the Father by being as He is. You'll only be able to access the guidance of this field of intention by being as it is. Stress, anxiety, and depression will be lifted from you with the assistance of that same force that created you. If it can create worlds out of nothing, and you out of nothing, surely the removal of some stress isn't such a big task. I believe that God's desire for you is that you not only know joy, but that you become it.

Step 9: Practice being in silence and meditation.

Nothing relieves stress, depression, anxiety, and all forms of low-energy emotions like silence and meditation. Here, you make conscious contact with your Source and cleanse your connecting link to intention. Take time every day for moments of quiet contemplation, and make meditation a part of your stress-reducing ritual.

Step 10: Stay in a state of gratitude and awe.

Go on a rampage of appreciation for all that you have, all that you are, and all that you observe. Gratitude is the tenth step in every ten-step program for manifesting your intentions, because it's the surest way to stop the incessant inner dialogue that leads you away from the joy and perfection of the Source. You can't feel stressed and appreciative at the same time.

Dr. Wayne Dyer was a best-selling author, writing over 40 books over a 40-year period. Find out more at: https://www.DrWayneDyer.com/

Dr. Dyer has numerous inspirational videos available for free on You Tube, including:

Four Hours of Wayne Dyer Motivation
https://www.youtube.com/watch?v=CjOvWYcpRaU

Making the Shift
https://www.youtube.com/watch?v=9cwZR4XDmX4&t=16s

Choose Your Own Greatness:
https://www.youtube.com/watch?v=fSzVSPnciSo

About the Author of this Book

Rodney Krafka is the author of this manual. He is a Founder and Deacon of North Shore Universal Church. He also works as the Director of Arbor Assets (www.ArborAssets.com), a U.S. based microfinance company operating in Central America. He lives in Seattle, Washington.

About NSUC and OrdainMinister.com

North Shore Universal Church (NSUC) is a non-denominational church based out of Seattle, Washington, and operating online at OrdainMinister.com. NSUC ordains people for free so they can conduct weddings and marriage ceremonies for friends, family, or as a paid marketable service. This open and inclusive attitude has been handed down through our Unitarian faith tradition and upheld throughout our church practices and endeavors.

NSUC members are united by a quest for spiritual growth, believing that this growth is the end goal, rather than obedience to a religious code. Due to the open nature of Unitarian Universalism, the theology incorporates ideas from many different religions and philosophies. Followers are free to believe whatever they choose spiritually, and so even atheists are accepted into the fold.

Because of this Unitarian belief in freedom of thought, the theology does not have any one official creed. Instead, the

Unitarian Universalist Association suggests Seven Principles which are paraphrased as follows.

Seven Principles of Unitarian Universalism

1. Respect for the value and dignity of every individual;
2. Fairness, empathy, and justness in human interaction;
3. Acceptance of all beliefs and encouragement towards personal spiritual growth;
4. Liberty to conduct a personal search for spiritual meaning;
5. The right to a democratic method in each congregation and in the world at large;
6. Pursuit of a peaceful world, with justice and freedom for every human;
7. Respect the interconnected web of the Universe;

Please consider taking the time to review our church website (www.OrdainMinister.com) where you can find our State Law Library Database where we maintain our complete collection of all marriage state laws from all U.S. states. Please also find our "Mission Outreach" tab, which includes materials for emotional and psychological support, stress management, as well as a brief discussion about our humanitarian work with Arbor Assets.

About Arbor Assets

Arbor Assets is an international microfinance company that also acts as NSUC's charity partner in conducting the church's humanitarian outreach. Arbor Assets contributes financial and knowledge-based resources to assist poor, rural communities in Honduras and Nicaragua. Founded in 2009, they are a U.S. 501(c)3 non-profit organization based out of Lincoln, Nebraska. While principally a micro-lending company, they also make strategic, capacity-expanding grants to partner organizations, usually in terms of additional education, equipment, or materials.

Find Arbor Assets online at: www.ArborAssets.com.

Support Arbor Assets by shopping on Amazon.com.

Find Arbor Assets as an officially registered charity participating in the AmazonSmile Program. Provide much-needed support and microfinance opportunities in Central America simply by shopping on Amazon.com. You shop, Amazon gives 0.5% of their money per every purchase - a half cent for every dollar you spend – as a donation to Arbor Assets.

Find Arbor Assets in the AmazonSmile[4] directory, or navigate directly to their organization profile and opt for immediate support by typing in this link: https://smile.amazon.com/ch/27-1154262

---

[4] AmazonSmile (smile.amazon.com) is the same Amazon.com you already know - with the same exact products, prices, service and shopping features as Amazon.com. The benefit is that when you register on AmazonSmile, the AmazonSmile Foundation will donate 0.5% of the listed purchase price of eligible products to the charitable organization of your choice (the donation money comes out of *their pockets, not yours*).

State Laws at a Glance

Alabama Code - Title 30 Marital and Domestic Relations - Chapter 1: Marriage § Section 30-1-7

(a) Generally. Marriages may be solemnized by any licensed minister of the gospel in regular communion with the Christian church or society of which the minister is a member; by an active or retired judge of the Supreme Court, Court of Criminal Appeals, Court of Civil Appeals, any circuit court, or any district court within this state; by a judge of any federal court; or by an active or retired judge of probate. (b) Pastor of religious society; clerk of society to maintain register of marriages; register, etc., deemed presumptive evidence of fact. Marriage may also be solemnized by the pastor of any religious society according to the rules ordained or custom established by such society. The clerk or keeper of the minutes of each society shall keep a register and enter therein a particular account of all marriages solemnized by the society, which register, or a sworn copy thereof, is presumptive evidence of the fact. (c) Quakers, Mennonites, or other religious societies. The people called Mennonites, Quakers, or any other Christian society having similar rules or regulations, may solemnize marriage according to their forms by consent of the parties, published and declared before the congregation assembled for public worship.

Alaska Code - Title 25: Marital and Domestic Relations - Chapter 5: Alaska Marriage Code - Article 5: Solemnization § Sec. 25.05.261

Who may solemnize: (a) Marriages may be solemnized (1) by a minister, priest, or rabbi of any church or congregation in the state, or by a commissioned officer of the Salvation Army, or by the principal officer or elder of recognized churches or congregations that traditionally do not have regular ministers, priests, or rabbis, anywhere within the state; (2) by a marriage commissioner or judicial officer of the state anywhere within the jurisdiction of the commissioner or officer; or (3) before or in any religious organization or congregation according to the established ritual or form commonly practiced in the organization or congregation. (b) This section may not be construed to waive the requirements for obtaining a marriage license. Sec. 25.05.271. Duty of officiating person before ceremony. The officiating person shall determine that the parties presenting themselves to be married are the parties named in the license. If the officiating person knows of a legal impediment to the marriage, the officiating person may not perform the ceremony.

Arizona Revised Statutes - Title 25: Marital and Domestic Regulations - Chapter 1: Marriage - Article 3: Marriage License, Ceremony and Record § 25-124

A. The following are authorized to solemnize marriages between persons who are authorized to marry: 1. Duly licensed or ordained clergymen. 2. Judges of courts of record. 3. Municipal court judges. 4. Justices of the peace. 5. Justices of the United States supreme court. 6. Judges of courts of appeals, district courts and courts that are created by an act of Congress if the judges are entitled to hold office during good behavior. 7. Bankruptcy court and tax court judges. 8. United States magistrate judges. 9. Judges of the Arizona court of military appeals. B. For the purposes of this section, "licensed or ordained clergymen" includes ministers, elders or other persons who by the customs, rules and regulations of a religious society or sect are authorized or permitted to solemnize marriages or to officiate at marriage ceremonies.

Arkansas Code - Title 9: Family Law - Subtitle 2: Domestic Relations - Chapter 11: Marriage - Subchapter 2: License and Ceremony § 9-11-213

(a) For the purpose of being registered and perpetuating the evidence thereof, marriage shall be solemnized only by the following persons: (1) The Governor; (2) Any former justice of the Supreme Court; (3) Any judges of the courts of record within this state, including any former judge of a court of record who served at least four (4) years or more; (4) Any justice of the peace, including any former justice of the peace who served at least two (2) terms since the passage of Arkansas Constitution, Amendment 55; (5) Any regularly ordained minister or priest of any religious sect or denomination; (6) The mayor of any city or town; (7) Any official appointed for that purpose by the quorum court of the county where the marriage is to be solemnized; or (8) Any elected district court judge and any former municipal or district court judge who served at least four (4) years. (b) (1) Marriages solemnized through the traditional rite of the Religious Society of Friends, more commonly known as Quakers, are recognized as valid to all intents and purposes the same as marriages otherwise contracted and solemnized in accordance with law. (2) The functions, duties, and liabilities of a party solemnizing marriage, as set forth in the marriage laws of this state, in the case of marriages solemnized through the traditional marriage rite of the Religious Society of Friends shall be incumbent upon the clerk of the congregation or, in his or her absence, his or her duly designated alternate.

California Law - Family Code - Division 3 - Marriage - Part 3 - Section 400

(a) Although marriage is a personal relation arising out of a civil, and not a religious, contract, a marriage may be solemnized by a priest, minister, rabbi, or authorized person of any religious denomination who is 18 years of age or older. A person authorized by this subdivision shall not be required to solemnize a marriage that is contrary to the tenets of his or her faith. Any refusal to solemnize a marriage under this subdivision, either by an individual or by a religious denomination, shall not affect the tax-exempt status of any entity. (b) Consistent with Section 94.5 of the Penal Code and provided that any compensation received is reasonable, including payment of actual expenses, a marriage may also be solemnized by any of the following persons: (1) A judge or retired judge, commissioner of civil marriages or retired commissioner of civil marriages, commissioner or retired commissioner, or assistant commissioner of a court of record in this state. (2) A judge or magistrate who has resigned from office. (3) Any of the following judges or magistrates of the United States: (A) A justice or retired justice of the United States Supreme Court. (B) A judge or retired judge of a court of appeals, a district court, or a court created by an act of the United States Congress the judges of which are entitled to hold office during good behavior. (C) A judge or retired judge of a bankruptcy court or a tax court. (D) A United States magistrate or retired magistrate. (c) Except as provided in subdivision (d), a marriage may also be solemnized by any of the following persons who are 18 years of age or older: (1) A Member of the Legislature or constitutional officer of this state or a Member of Congress of the United States who represents a district within this state, or a former Member of the Legislature or constitutional officer of this state or a former Member of Congress of the United States who represented a district within this state. (2) A person that holds or formerly held an elected office of a city, county, or city and county. (3) A city clerk of a charter city or serving in accordance with subdivision (b) of Section 36501 of the Government Code, while that person holds office. (d) (1) A person listed in subdivision (c) shall not accept compensation for solemnizing a marriage while holding office. (2) A person listed in subdivision (c) shall not solemnize a marriage pursuant to this section if they have been removed from office due to committing an offense or have been convicted of an offense that involves moral turpitude, dishonesty, or fraud.

Colorado Revised Statutes - Title 14: Domestic Matters - Article 2: Marriage and Rights of Married Women - Part 1: Uniform Marriage Act § 14-2-109

(1) A marriage may be solemnized by a judge of a court, by a court magistrate, by a retired judge of a court, by a public official whose powers include solemnization of marriages, by the parties to the marriage, or in accordance with any mode of solemnization recognized by any religious denomination or Indian nation or tribe. Either the person solemnizing the marriage or, if no individual acting alone solemnized the marriage, a party to the marriage shall complete the marriage certificate form and forward it to the county clerk and recorder within sixty days after the solemnization. Any person who fails to forward the marriage certificate to the county clerk and recorder as required by this section shall be required to pay a late fee in an amount of not less than twenty dollars. An additional five-dollar late fee may be assessed for each additional day of failure to comply with the forwarding requirements of this subsection (1) up to a maximum of fifty dollars. For purposes of determining whether a late fee shall be assessed pursuant to this subsection (1), the date of forwarding shall be deemed to be the date of postmark. (2) If a party to a marriage is unable to be present at the solemnization, such party may authorize in writing a third

person to act as such party's proxy. If the person solemnizing the marriage is satisfied that the absent party is unable to be present and has consented to the marriage, such person may solemnize the marriage by proxy. If such person is not satisfied, the parties may petition the district court for an order permitting the marriage to be solemnized by proxy. (3) Upon receipt of the marriage certificate, the county clerk and recorder shall register the marriage.

Connecticut General Statutes - Volume 12 - Title 46b: Family Law - Chapter 815e: Marriage § Sec. 46b-22

(a) Persons authorized to solemnize marriages in this state include (1) all judges and retired judges, either elected or appointed, including federal judges and judges of other states who may legally join persons in marriage in their jurisdictions, (2) family support magistrates, state referees and justices of the peace who are appointed in Connecticut, and (3) all ordained or licensed members of the clergy, belonging to this state or any other state, as long as they continue in the work of the ministry. All marriages solemnized according to the forms and usages of any religious denomination in this state, including marriages witnessed by a duly constituted Spiritual Assembly of the Baha'is, are valid. All marriages attempted to be celebrated by any other person are void. (b) No public official legally authorized to issue marriage licenses may join persons in marriage under authority of a license issued by himself, or his assistant or deputy; nor may any such assistant or deputy join persons in marriage under authority of a license issued by such public official. (c) Any person violating any provision of this section shall be fined not more than fifty dollars.

Delaware Code - Title 13: Domestic Relations - Chapter 1: Marriage - Subchapter I: General Provisions § § 106

(a) A clergyperson or minister of any religion, current and former Judges of this State's Supreme Court, Superior Court, Family Court, Court of Chancery, Court of Common Pleas, Justice of the Peace Court, federal Judges, federal Magistrates, clerks of the peace of various counties and current and former judges from other jurisdictions with written authorization by the clerk of the peace from the county in Delaware where the ceremony is to be performed may solemnize marriages between persons who may lawfully enter into the matrimonial relation. The Clerk of the Peace in each county for good cause being shown may: (1) Allow by written permit within that Clerk's respective county, any duly sworn member of another state's judiciary, to solemnize marriages in the State between persons who may lawfully enter into the matrimonial relation. (2) Allow by written permit within that Clerk's respective county, the Clerk of the Peace from another county within the State to solemnize marriages in the State between persons who may lawfully enter into the matrimonial relation. Within the limits of any incorporated municipality, the Mayor thereof may solemnize marriages between persons who may lawfully enter into matrimonial relation. Marriages shall be solemnized in the presence of at least 2 reputable witnesses who shall sign the certificate of marriage as prescribed by this chapter. Marriages may also be solemnized or contracted according to the forms and usages of any religious society. No marriage shall be solemnized or contracted without the production of a license issued pursuant to this chapter. (b) For purposes of this section, the words "resident of this State" shall include the son or daughter of a person who has been domiciled within the State for 1 year or more, notwithstanding the actual place of residence of the son or daughter immediately prior to the date of the marriage. (c) In the case of absence or disability of the duly elected Clerk of the Peace, the chief deputy or, if there is no chief deputy, a deputy employed in the office of the Clerk of the Peace, shall be authorized to solemnize marriages. (d) Whoever, not being authorized by this section, solemnizes a marriage, shall be fined $100, and in default of the payment of such fine shall be imprisoned not more than 30 days, and such marriage shall be void, unless it is in other respects lawful and is consummated with the full belief of either of the parties in its validity.

Florida Statutes - Title XLIII: Domestic Relations - Chapter 741: Marriage; Domestic Violence § 741.07

(1) All regularly ordained ministers of the gospel or elders in communion with some church, or other ordained clergy, and all judicial officers, including retired judicial officers, clerks of the circuit courts, and notaries public of this state may solemnize the rights of matrimonial contract, under the regulations prescribed by law. Nothing in this section shall

make invalid a marriage which was solemnized by any member of the clergy, or as otherwise provided by law prior to July 1, 1978. (2)Any marriage which may be had and solemnized among the people called Quakers, or Friends, in the manner and form used or practiced in their societies, according to their rites and ceremonies, shall be good and valid in law; and wherever the words minister and elder are used in this chapter, they shall be held to include all of the persons connected with the Society of Friends, or Quakers, who perform or have charge of the marriage ceremony according to their rites and ceremonies.

Georgia Code Annotated - Title 19: Domestic Relations - Chapter 3: Marriage Generally - Article 2: License and Ceremony § § 19-3-42

A marriage which is valid in other respects and supposed by the parties to be valid shall not be affected by want of authority in the minister, Governor or any former Governor of this state, judge, city recorder, magistrate, or other person to solemnize the same; nor shall such objection be heard from one party who has fraudulently induced the other to believe that the marriage was legal.

The license shall be directed to any judge, including judges of state and federal courts of record in this state, city recorder, magistrate, minister, or other person of any religious society or sect authorized by the rules of such society to perform the marriage ceremony; such license shall authorize the marriage of the persons therein named and require the judge, city recorder, magistrate, minister, or other authorized person to return the license to the judge of the probate court with the certificate thereon as to the fact and date of marriage within 30 days after the date of the marriage. The license with the return thereon shall be recorded by the judge in a book kept by such judge for that purpose.

Hawaii Revised Statutes - Division 1: Government - Title 31: Family - Chapter 572: Marriage - Part 1: Requisites, Procedures; § § 572-12

A license to solemnize marriages may be issued to, and the marriage rite may be performed and solemnized by any minister, priest, or officer of any religious denomination or society who has been ordained or is authorized to solemnize marriages according to the usages of such denomination or society, or any religious society not having clergy but providing solemnization in accordance with the rules and customs of that society, or any justice or judge or magistrate, active or retired, of a state or federal court in the State, upon presentation to such person or society of a license to marry, as prescribed by this chapter. Such person or society may receive the price stipulated by the parties or the gratification tendered.

Idaho Statutes - Title 32: Domestic Relations - Chapter 3: Solemnization of Marriage § 32-303

Marriage may be solemnized by any of the following Idaho officials: a current or retired justice of the supreme court, a current or retired court of appeals judge, a current or retired district judge, the current or a former governor, the current lieutenant governor, a current or retired magistrate of the district court, a current mayor or by any of the following: a current federal judge, a current tribal judge of an Idaho Indian tribe or other tribal official approved by an official act of an Idaho Indian tribe or priest or minister of the gospel of any denomination. To be a retired justice of the supreme court, court of appeals judge, district judge or magistrate judge of the district court, for the purpose of solemnizing marriages, a person shall have served in one (1) of those offices and shall be receiving a retirement benefit from either the judges retirement system or the public employee retirement system for service in the Idaho judiciary.

Illinois Compiled Statutes - Rights and Remedies - Chapter 750. Families - 5. Illinois Marriage and Dissolution of Marriage Act - Part II. Marriage § Sec. 209

(a) A marriage may be solemnized by a judge of a court of record, by a retired judge of a court of record, unless the retired judge was removed from office by the Judicial Inquiry Board, except that a retired judge shall not receive any compensation from the State, a county or any unit of local government in return for the solemnization of a marriage and there shall be no effect upon any pension benefits conferred by the Judges Retirement System of Illinois, by a judge of the Court of Claims, by a county clerk in counties having 2,000,000 or more inhabitants, by a public official whose powers include solemnization of marriages, or in accordance with the prescriptions of any religious denomination, Indian Nation or Tribe or Native Group, provided that when such prescriptions require an officiant, the officiant be in good standing with his religious denomination, Indian Nation or Tribe or Native Group. Either the person solemnizing the marriage, or, if no individual acting alone solemnized the marriage, both parties to the marriage, shall complete the marriage certificate form and forward it to the county clerk within 10 days after such marriage is solemnized. (b) The solemnization of the marriage is not invalidated by the fact that the person solemnizing the marriage was not legally qualified to solemnize it, if either party to the marriage believed him to be so qualified or by the fact that the marriage was inadvertently solemnized in a county in Illinois other than the county where the license was issued.

Indiana Code - Title 31: Family Law and Juvenile Law - Article 11: Marriage - Chapter 6: Authority to Solemnize Marriages § IC 31-11-6-1

Marriages may be solemnized by any of the following: (1) A member of the clergy of a religious organization (even if the cleric does not perform religious functions for an individual congregation), such as a minister of the gospel, a priest, a bishop, an archbishop, or a rabbi. (2) A judge. (3) A mayor, within the mayor's county. (4) A clerk or a clerk-treasurer of a city or town, within a county in which the city or town is located. (5) A clerk of the circuit court. (6) The Friends Church, in accordance with the rules of the Friends Church. (7) The German Baptists, in accordance with the rules of their society.

(8) The Bahai faith, in accordance with the rules of the Bahai faith. (9) The Church of Jesus Christ of Latter Day Saints, in accordance with the rules of the Church of Jesus Christ of Latter Day Saints. (10) An imam of a masjid (mosque), in accordance with the rules of the religion of Islam.

Iowa Code - Title XV. Judicial Branch and Judicial Procedures - Subtitle 1. Domestic Relations - Chapter 595. Marriage § 595.1

Marriages may be solemnized by: (1) A judge of the supreme court, court of appeals, or district court, including a district associate judge, associate juvenile judge, or a judicial magistrate, and including a senior judge as defined in section 602.9202, subsection 3. (2) A person ordained or designated as a leader of the person's religious faith.

Kansas Statutes - Chapter 23: Domestic Relations - Article 1: Marriage § 23-104a

(a) Marriage may be validly solemnized and contracted in this state, after a license has been issued for the marriage, in the following manner: By the mutual declarations of the two parties to be joined in marriage, made before an authorized officiating person and in the presence of at least two competent witnesses over 18 years of age, other than the officiating person, that they take each other as husband and wife. (b) The following are authorized to be officiating persons: (1) Any currently ordained clergyman or religious authority of any religious denomination or society; (2) any licentiate of a denominational body or an appointee of any bishop serving as the regular clergyman of any church of the denomination to which the licentiate or appointee belongs, if not restrained from so doing by the discipline of that church or denomination; (3) any judge or justice of a court of record; (4) any municipal judge of a city of this state; and (5) any retired judge or justice of a court of record. (c) The two parties themselves, by mutual declarations that they take each other as husband and wife, in accordance with the customs, rules and regulations of any religious society, denomination or sect to which either of the parties belong, may be married without an authorized officiating person.

Kentucky Revised Statutes - Title XXXV: Domestic Relations - Chapter 402: Marriage – Solemnization § 402.050

(1) Marriage shall be solemnized only by: (a) Ministers of the gospel or priests of any denomination in regular communion with any religious society; (b) Justices and judges of the Court of Justice, retired justices and judges of the Court of Justice except those removed for cause or convicted of a felony, county judges/executive, and such justices of the peace and fiscal court commissioners as the Governor or the county judge/executive authorizes; or (c) A religious society that has no officiating minister or priest and whose usage is to solemnize marriage at the usual place of worship and by consent given in the presence of the society, if either party belongs to the society. (2) At least two (2) persons, in addition

to the parties and the person solemnizing the marriage, shall be present at every marriage.

Louisiana Revised Statutes - Title 9: Civil Code-Ancillaries - Code Title IV: Husband and Wife - Chapter 1: Marriage General Principles - Part I. Officiants § §202

A marriage ceremony may be performed by: (1) A priest, minister, rabbi, clerk of the Religious Society of Friends, or any clergyman of any religious sect, who is authorized by the authorities of his religion to perform marriages, and who is registered to perform marriages; (2) A state judge or justice of the peace.

Maine Revised Statutes - Title 19-A: Domestic Relations - Part 2: Married Persons - Chapter 23: Marriage - Subchapter 1: General Provisions § § 655

1. Persons authorized to solemnize marriages. The following may solemnize marriages in this State: A. If a resident of this State: (1) A justice or judge; (2) A lawyer admitted to the Maine Bar; or (4) A notary public under Title 4, chapter 19; and [2001, c. 574, §6 (AMD).] B. Whether a resident or nonresident of this State and whether or not a citizen of the United States: (1) An ordained minister of the gospel; (2) A cleric engaged in the service of the religious body to which the cleric belongs; or (3) A person licensed to preach by an association of ministers,

religious seminary or ecclesiastical body. [1995, c. 694, Pt. B, §2 (NEW); 1995, c. 694, Pt. E, §2 (AFF).] [2001, c. 574, §6 (AMD).] 2. Enforcement. The State Registrar of Vital Statistics shall enforce this section as far as it comes within the state registrar's power and shall notify the district attorney of the county in which the penalty should be enforced of the facts that have come to the state registrar's knowledge. Upon receipt of this notice, the district attorney shall prosecute the person who violated this section. [1995, c. 694, Pt. B, §2 (NEW); 1995, c. 694, Pt. E, §2 (AFF).]

Maryland Code - Family Law - Title 2. Marriage - Subtitle 4: Licensing and Performance § § 2-406

(a) Authorized officials.- (1) In this subsection, "judge" means: (i) a judge of the District Court, a circuit court, the Court of Special Appeals, or the Court of Appeals; (ii) a judge approved under Article IV, § 3A of the Maryland Constitution and § 1-302 of the Courts Article for recall and assignment to the District Court, a circuit court, the Court of Special Appeals, or the Court of Appeals; (iii) a judge of a United States District Court, a United States Court of Appeals, or the United States Tax Court; or (iv) a judge of a state court if the judge is active or retired but eligible for recall. (2) A marriage ceremony may be performed in this State by: (i) any official of a religious order or body authorized by the rules and customs of that order or body to perform a marriage ceremony; (ii) any clerk; (iii) any deputy clerk designated by the county administrative judge of the circuit court for the county; or (iv) a judge. (b) Period during which ceremony may be performed. Within 6 months after a license becomes effective, any authorized official may perform the marriage ceremony of the individuals named in the license. (c) Performance by unauthorized individual prohibited; penalty. (1) An individual may not perform a marriage ceremony unless the individual is authorized to perform a marriage ceremony under subsection (a) of this section. (2) An individual who violates this subsection is guilty of a misdemeanor and on conviction is subject to a fine of $500. (d) Performance between individuals within prohibited degrees prohibited; penalty. (1) An individual may not knowingly perform a marriage ceremony between individuals who are prohibited from marrying under § 2-202 of this title. (2) An individual who violates the provisions of this subsection is guilty of a misdemeanor and on conviction is subject to a fine of $500. (e) Performance without license prohibited; penalty. (1) An individual may not perform a marriage ceremony without a license that is effective under this subtitle. (2) An individual who violates the provisions of this subsection is guilty of a misdemeanor and on conviction is subject to a fine not exceeding $500. (f) Ceremony performed by a clerk or deputy clerk. The county administrative judge of the circuit court for the county shall designate: (1) when and where the clerk or deputy clerk may perform a marriage ceremony; and (2) the form of the marriage ceremony to be recited by the clerk or deputy clerk and the parties being married. (g) Forms of religious ceremonies. This section does not affect the right of any religious denomination to perform a marriage ceremony in accordance with the rules and customs of the denomination.

Massachusetts General Laws - Part II: Real and Personal Property and Domestic Relations - Title III: Domestic Relations - Chapter 207: Marriage § Section 38

A marriage may be solemnized in any place within the commonwealth by the following persons who are residents of the commonwealth: a duly ordained minister of the gospel in good and regular standing with his church or denomination, including an ordained deacon in The United Methodist Church or in the Roman Catholic Church; a commissioned cantor or duly ordained rabbi of the Jewish faith; by a justice of the peace if he is also clerk or assistant clerk of a city or town, or a registrar or assistant registrar, or a clerk or assistant clerk of a court or a clerk or assistant clerk of the senate or house of representatives, by a justice of the peace if he has been designated as provided in the following section and has received a certificate of designation and has qualified thereunder; an authorized representative of a Spiritual Assembly of the Baha'is in accordance with the usage of their community; a priest or minister of the Buddhist religion; a minister in fellowship with the Unitarian Universalist Association and ordained by a local church; a leader of an Ethical Culture Society which is duly established in the commonwealth and recognized by the American Ethical Union and who is duly appointed and in good and regular standing with the American Ethical Union; the Imam of the Orthodox Islamic religion; and, it may be solemnized in a regular or special meeting for worship conducted by or under the oversight of a Friends or Quaker Monthly Meeting in accordance with the usage of their Society; and, it may be solemnized by a duly ordained nonresident minister of the gospel if he is a pastor of a church or denomination duly established in the commonwealth and who is in good and regular standing as a minister of such church or denomination, including an ordained deacon in The United Methodist Church or in the Roman Catholic Church; and, it may be solemnized according to the usage of any other church or religious organization which shall have complied with the provisions of the second paragraph of this section. Churches and other religious organizations shall file in the office of the state secretary information relating to persons recognized or licensed as aforesaid, and relating to usages of such organizations, in such form and at such times as the secretary may require.

Michigan Compiled Laws - Chapter 551: Marriage § 551.7

(1) Marriages may be solemnized by any of the following: (a) A judge of the district court, in the district in which the judge is serving. (b) A district court magistrate, in the district in which the magistrate serves. (c) A municipal judge, in the city in which the judge is serving or in a township over which a municipal court has jurisdiction under section 9928 of the revised judicature act of 1961, 1961 PA 236, MCL 600.9928. (d) A judge of probate, in the county or probate court district in which the judge is serving. (e) A judge of a federal court. (f) A mayor of a city, anywhere in a county in which that city is located. (g) A county clerk in the county in which the clerk serves, or in another county with the written authorization of the clerk of the other county. (h) For a county having more

than 2,000,000 inhabitants, an employee of the county clerk's office designated by the county clerk, in the county in which the clerk serves. (i) A minister of the gospel or cleric or religious practitioner, anywhere in the state, if the minister or cleric or religious practitioner is ordained or authorized to solemnize marriages according to the usages of the denomination. (j) A minister of the gospel or cleric or religious practitioner, anywhere in the state, if the minister or cleric or religious practitioner is not a resident of this state but is authorized to solemnize marriages under the laws of the state in which the minister or cleric or religious practitioner resides. (2) A person authorized by this act to solemnize a marriage shall keep proper records and make returns as required by section 4 of 1887 PA 128, MCL 551.104. (3) If a mayor of a city solemnizes a marriage, the mayor shall charge and collect a fee to be determined by the council of that city, which shall be paid to the city treasurer and deposited in the general fund of the city at the end of the month. (4) If the county clerk or, in a county having more than 2,000,000 inhabitants, an employee of the clerk's office designated by the county clerk solemnizes a marriage, the county clerk shall charge and collect a fee to be determined by the commissioners of the county in which the clerk serves. The fee shall be paid to the treasurer for the county in which the clerk serves and deposited in the general fund of that county at the end of the month.

Minnesota Statutes - Chapter 517: Marriage § 517.04

Marriages may be solemnized throughout the state by an individual who has attained the age of 21 years and is a judge of a court of record, a retired judge of a court of record, a court administrator, a retired court administrator with the approval of the chief judge of the judicial district, a former court commissioner who is employed by the court system or is acting pursuant to an order of the chief judge of the commissioner's judicial district, the residential school administrators of the Minnesota State Academy for the Deaf and the Minnesota State Academy for the Blind, a licensed or ordained minister of any religious denomination, or by any mode recognized in section 517.18.

517.05 Credentials of minister: Ministers of any religious denomination, before they are authorized to solemnize a marriage, shall file a copy of their credentials of license or ordination with the court administrator of the district court of a county in this state, who shall record the same and give a certificate thereof. The place where the credentials are recorded shall be endorsed upon and recorded with each certificate of marriage granted by a minister.

Mississippi Code - Title 93: Domestic Relations - Chapter 1: Marriage § § 93-1-17

Any minister of the gospel ordained according to the rules of his church or society, in good standing; any Rabbi or other spiritual leader of any other religious body authorized under the rules of such religious body to solemnize rites of matrimony and being in good standing; any judge of the Supreme Court, Court of Appeals, circuit court, chancery court or county court may solemnize the rites of matrimony between any persons anywhere within this state who shall produce a license granted as herein directed. Justice court judges and members of the boards of supervisors may likewise solemnize the rites of matrimony within their respective counties. Any marriages performed by a mayor of a municipality prior to March 14, 1994 are valid provided such marriages satisfy the requirements of Section 93-1-18.

Missouri Revised Statutes - Title XXX: Domestic Relations - Chapter 451: Marriage, Marriage Contracts, and Rights of Married Women § 451.100

Marriages may be solemnized by any clergyman, either active or retired, who is in good standing with any church or synagogue in this state. Marriages may also be solemnized, without compensation, by any judge, including a municipal judge. Marriages may also be solemnized by a religious society, religious institution, or religious organization of this state, according to the regulations and customs of the society, institution or organization, when either party to the marriage to be solemnized is a member of such society, institution or organization.

Montana Code Annotated - Title 40: Family Law - Chapter 1: Marriage - Part 3: Solemnization § 40-1 301

(1) A marriage may be solemnized by a judge of a court of record, by a public official whose powers include solemnization of marriages, by a mayor, city judge, or justice of the peace, by a tribal judge, or in accordance with any mode of solemnization recognized by any religious denomination, Indian nation or tribe, or native group. Either the person solemnizing the marriage or, if no individual acting alone solemnized the marriage, a party to the marriage shall complete the marriage certificate form and forward it to the clerk of the district court. (2) If a party to a marriage is unable to be present at the solemnization, the party may authorize in writing a third person to act as proxy. If the person solemnizing the marriage is satisfied that the absent party is unable to be present and has consented to the marriage, the person may solemnize the marriage by proxy. If the person solemnizing the marriage is not satisfied, the parties may petition the district court for an order permitting the marriage to be solemnized by proxy. (3) The solemnization of the marriage is not invalidated by the fact that the person solemnizing the marriage was not legally qualified to solemnize it if either party to the marriage believed that person to be qualified. (4) One party to a proxy marriage must be a member of the armed forces of the United States on federal active duty or a resident of Montana at the time of application for a license and certificate pursuant to 40-1-202. One party or a legal representative shall appear before the clerk of court and pay the marriage license fee. For the purposes of this subsection, residency must be determined in accordance with 1-1-215.

Nebraska Revised Statutes - Chapter 42: Husband and Wife § 42-108

Every judge, retired judge, clerk magistrate, or retired clerk magistrate, and every preacher of the gospel authorized by the usages of the church to which he or she belongs to solemnize marriages, may perform the marriage ceremony in this state. Every such person performing the marriage ceremony shall make a return of his or her proceedings in the premises, showing the names and residences of at least two witnesses who were present at such marriage. The return shall be made to the county clerk who issued the license within fifteen days after such marriage has been performed. The county clerk shall record the return or cause it to be recorded in the same book where the marriage license is recorded.

Nevada Revised Statutes - Title 11: Domestic Relations - Chapter 122: Marriage - Certificates of Permission to Perform Marriages § NRS 122.062

1. Any licensed, ordained or appointed minister or other person authorized to solemnize a marriage in good standing within his or her church or religious organization, or either of them, incorporated, organized or established in this State, may join together as husband and wife persons who present a marriage license obtained from any county clerk of the State, if the minister or other person authorized to solemnize a marriage first obtains a certificate of permission to perform

North Shore Universal Church

marriages as provided in NRS 122.062 to 122.073, inclusive. The fact that a minister or other person authorized to solemnize a marriage is retired does not disqualify him or her from obtaining a certificate of permission to perform marriages if, before retirement, the minister or other person authorized to solemnize a marriage had active charge of a church or religious organization for a period of at least 3 years. 2. A temporary replacement for a licensed, ordained or appointed minister or other person authorized to solemnize a marriage certified pursuant to NRS 122.062 to 122.073, inclusive, may solemnize marriages pursuant to subsection 1 during such time as he or she may be authorized to do so by the county clerk in the county in which he or she is a temporary replacement, for a period not to exceed 90 days. The minister or other person authorized to solemnize a marriage whom he or she temporarily replaces shall provide him or her with a written authorization which states the period during which it is effective. 3. Any chaplain who is assigned to duty in this State by the Armed Forces of the United States may solemnize marriages if the chaplain obtains a certificate of permission to perform marriages from the county clerk of the county in which his or her duty station is located. The county clerk shall issue such a certificate to a chaplain upon proof of his or her military status as a chaplain and of his or her assignment. 4. A county clerk may authorize a licensed, ordained or appointed minister or other person authorized to solemnize a marriage whose residence and church or religious organization is in another state or who is retired, if his or her service was as described in subsection 1, to perform marriages in the county if the county clerk is satisfied that the minister or other person authorized to solemnize a marriage is in good standing with his or her church or religious organization pursuant to this section.

The authorization must be in writing and need not be filed with any other public officer. A separate authorization is required for each marriage performed. Such a minister or other person authorized to solemnize a marriage may perform not more than five marriages in this State in any calendar year and must acknowledge that he or she is subject to the jurisdiction of the county clerk with respect to the provisions of this chapter governing the conduct of ministers or other persons authorized to solemnize a marriage to the same extent as if he or she were a minister or other person authorized to solemnize a marriage residing in this State.

New Hampshire Statutes - Title 63: Domestic Relations - Chapter 457: Marriages § Section 457:31

A marriage may be solemnized in the following manner: I. In a civil ceremony by a justice of the peace as commissioned by the state and by judges of the United States appointed pursuant to Article III of the United States Constitution, by bankruptcy judges appointed pursuant to Article I of the United States Constitution, or by United States magistrate judges appointed pursuant to federal law; or II. In a religious ceremony by any minister of the gospel in the state who has been ordained according to the usage of his or her denomination, resides in the state, and is in regular standing with the denomination; by any member of the clergy who is not ordained but is engaged in the service of the religious body to which he or she belongs, and who resides in the state, after being licensed therefor by the secretary of state; or within his or her parish, by any minister residing out of the state, but having a pastoral charge wholly or partly in this state.

New Jersey Permanent Statutes - Title 37: Marriages and Married Persons § 37:1-13

Each judge of the United States Court of Appeals for the Third Circuit, each judge of a federal district court, United States magistrate, judge of a municipal court, judge of the Superior Court, judge of a tax court, retired judge of the Superior Court or Tax Court, or judge of the Superior Court or Tax Court, the former County Court, the former County Juvenile and Domestic Relations Court, or the former County District Court who has resigned in good standing, surrogate of any county, county clerk and any mayor or the deputy mayor when authorized by the mayor, or chairman of any township committee or village president of this State, and every minister of every religion, are hereby authorized to solemnize marriages or civil unions between such persons as may lawfully enter into the matrimonial relation or civil union; and every religious society, institution or organization in this State may join together in marriage or civil union such persons according to the rules and customs of the society, institution or organization.

New Mexico Statutes Annotated - Chapter 40: Domestic Affairs - Article 1: Marriage in General § 40-1-2

A. A person may solemnize the contract of matrimony by means of an ordained clergyman or authorized representative of a federally recognized Indian tribe, without regard to the sect to which he may belong or the rites and customs he may practice. B. Judges, justices and magistrates of any of the courts established by the constitution of New Mexico, United States constitution, laws of the state or laws of the United States are civil magistrates having authority to solemnize contracts of matrimony. C. Civil magistrates solemnizing contracts of matrimony shall charge no fee therefor.

Laws of New York - DOM Domestic Relations - Article 3 - Section 11

§ 11. By whom a marriage must be solemnized. No marriage shall be valid unless solemnized by either: 1. A clergyman or minister of any religion, or by the senior leader, or any of the other leaders, of The Society for Ethical Culture in the city of New York, having its principal office in the borough of Manhattan, or by the leader of The Brooklyn Society for Ethical Culture, having its principal office in the borough of Brooklyn of the city of New York, or of the Westchester Ethical Society, having its principal office in Westchester county, or of the Ethical Culture Society of Long Island, having its principal office in Nassau county, or of the Riverdale-Yonkers Ethical Society having its principal office in Bronx county, or by the leader of any other Ethical Culture Society affiliated with the American

Ethical Union. 2. A mayor of a village, a county executive of a county, or a mayor, recorder, city magistrate, police justice or police magistrate of a city, a former mayor or the city clerk of a city of the first class of over one million inhabitants or any of his or her deputies or not more than four regular clerks, designated by him or her for such purpose as provided in section eleven-a of this chapter, except that in cities which contain more than one hundred thousand and less than one million inhabitants, a marriage shall be solemnized by the mayor, or police justice, and by no other officer of such city, except as provided in subdivisions one and three of this section. 3. A judge of the federal circuit court of appeals for the second circuit, a judge of a federal district court for the northern, southern, eastern or western district of New York, a judge of the United States court of international trade, a federal administrative law judge presiding in this state, a justice or judge of a court of the unified court system, a housing judge of the civil court of the city of New York, a retired justice or judge of the unified court system or a retired housing judge of the civil court of the city of New York certified pursuant to paragraph (k) of subdivision two of section two hundred twelve of the judiciary law, the clerk of the appellate division of the supreme court in each judicial department, a retired city clerk who served for more than ten years in such capacity in a city having a population of one million or more or a county clerk of a county wholly within cities having a population of one million or more; or, 4. A written contract of marriage signed by both parties and at least two witnesses, all of whom shall subscribe the same within this state, stating the place of residence of each of the parties and witnesses and the date and place of marriage, and acknowledged before a judge of a court of record of this state by the parties and witnesses in the manner required for the acknowledgment of a conveyance of real estate to entitle the same to be recorded. 5. Notwithstanding any other provision of this article, where either or both of the parties is under the age of eighteen years a marriage shall be solemnized only by those authorized in subdivision one of this section or by (1) the mayor of a city or village, or county executive of a county, or by (2) a judge of the federal circuit court of appeals for the second circuit, a judge of a federal district court for the northern, southern, eastern or western district of New York, a judge of the United States court of international trade, or a justice or a judge of a court of the unified court system, or by (3) a housing judge of the civil court of the city of New York, or by (4) a former mayor or the clerk of a city of the first class of over one million inhabitants or any of his or her deputies designated by him or her for such purposes as provided in section eleven-a of this chapter. 6. Notwithstanding any other provisions of this article to the contrary no marriage shall be solemnized by a public officer specified in this section, other than a judge of a federal district court for the northern, southern, eastern or western district of New York, a judge of the United States court of international trade, a federal administrative law judge presiding in this state, a judge or justice of the unified court system of this State, a housing judge of the civil court of the city of New York, or a retired judge or justice of the unified court system or a retired housing judge of the civil court certified pursuant to paragraph (k) of subdivision two of section two hundred twelve of the judiciary law, outside the territorial jurisdiction in which he or she was elected or appointed. Such a public officer, however, elected or appointed within the city of New York may solemnize a marriage anywhere within such city. 7. The term "clergyman" or "minister" when used in this article, shall include those defined in section two of the religious corporations law. The word "magistrate, " when so used, includes any person referred to in the second or third subdivision.

North Carolina General Statutes - Chapter 51: Marriage - Article 1: General Provisions § 51-1

A valid and sufficient marriage is created by the consent of a male and female person who may lawfully marry, presently to take each other as husband and wife, freely, seriously and plainly expressed by each in the presence of the other, either: (1) a. In the presence of an ordained minister of any religious denomination, a minister authorized by a church, or a magistrate; and b. With the consequent declaration by the minister or magistrate that the persons are husband and wife; or (2) In accordance with any mode of solemnization recognized by any religious denomination, or federally or State recognized Indian Nation or Tribe. Marriages solemnized before March 9, 1909, by ministers of the gospel licensed, but not ordained, are validated from their consummation.

North Dakota Century Code - Title 14: Domestic Relations and Person - Chapter 3: Marriage Contract § 14-03-09

Marriages may be solemnized by all judges of courts of record; municipal judges; recorders, unless the board of county commissioners designates a different official; ordained ministers of the gospel; priests; clergy licensed by recognized denominations pursuant to chapter 10-33; and by any person authorized by the rituals and practices of any religious persuasion.

Ohio Revised Code - Title XXXI: Domestic Relations - Children - Chapter 3031: Marriage § 3101.08

An ordained or licensed minister of any religious society or congregation within this state who is licensed to solemnize marriages, a judge of a county court in accordance with section 1907.18 of the Revised Code, a judge of a municipal court in accordance with section 1901.14 of the Revised Code, a probate judge in accordance with section 2101.27 of the Revised Code, the mayor of a municipal corporation in any county in which such municipal corporation wholly or partly lies, the superintendent of the state school for the deaf, or any religious society in conformity with the rules of its church, may join together as husband and wife any persons who are not prohibited by law from being joined in marriage.

Oklahoma Statutes - Title 43: Husband and Wife § §43-7

A. All marriages must be contracted by a formal ceremony performed or solemnized in the presence of at least two adult, competent persons as witnesses, by a judge or retired judge of any court in this state, or an ordained or authorized preacher or minister of the Gospel, priest or other ecclesiastical dignitary of any denomination who has been duly ordained or authorized by the church to which he or she belongs to preach the Gospel, or a rabbi and who is at least eighteen (18) years of age. B. 1. The judge shall place his or her order of appointment on file with the office of the court clerk of the county in which he or she resides. 2. The preacher, minister, priest, rabbi, or ecclesiastical dignitary who is a resident of this state shall have filed, in the office of the court clerk of the county in which he or she resides, a copy of the credentials or authority from his or her church or synagogue authorizing him or her to solemnize marriages. 3. The preacher, minister, priest, rabbi, or ecclesiastical dignitary who is not a resident of this state, but has complied with the laws of the state of which he or she is a resident, shall have filed once, in the office of the court clerk of the county in which he or she intends to perform or solemnize a marriage, a copy of the credentials or authority from his or her church or synagogue authorizing him or her to solemnize marriages. 4. The filing by resident or nonresident preachers, ministers, priests, rabbis, ecclesiastical dignitaries or judges shall be effective in and for all counties of this state; provided, no fee shall be charged for such recording. C. No person herein authorized to perform or solemnize a marriage ceremony shall do so unless the license issued therefor be first delivered into his or her possession nor unless he or she has good reason to believe the persons presenting themselves before him or her for marriage are the identical persons named in the license, and for whose marriage the same was issued, and that there is no legal objection or impediment to such marriage. D. Marriages between persons belonging to the society called Friends, or Quakers, the spiritual assembly of the Baha'is, or the Church of Jesus Christ of Latter Day Saints, which have no ordained minister, may be solemnized by the persons and in the manner prescribed by and practiced in any such society, church, or assembly.

Oregon Revised Statutes - Title 11: Domestic Relations - Chapter 106: Marriage; Domestic Partnership § 106.130

A marriage solemnized before any person professing to be a judicial officer of this state, a county clerk or a clergyperson of a religious congregation or organization therein is not void, nor shall the validity thereof be in any way affected, on account of any want of power or authority in such person, if such person was acting at the time in the office or the capacity of a person authorized to solemnize marriage and if such marriage is consummated with the belief on the part of the persons so married, or either of them, that they have been lawfully joined in marriage.

Pennsylvania Consolidated Statutes - Title 23: Domestic Relations - Part 2: Marriage - Chapter 15: Marriage Ceremony § § 1503

(a) General rule. The following are authorized to solemnize marriages between persons that produce a marriage license issued under this part: (1) A justice, judge or magisterial district judge of this Commonwealth. (2) A former or retired justice, judge or magisterial district judge of this Commonwealth who

North Shore Universal Church

is serving as a senior judge or senior magisterial district judge as provided or prescribed by law; or not serving as a senior judge or senior magisterial district judge but meets the following criteria: (i) has served as a magisterial district judge, judge or justice, whether or not continuously or on the same court, by election or appointment for an aggregate period equaling a full term of office; (ii) has not been defeated for reelection or retention; (iii) has not been convicted of, pleaded nolo contendere to or agreed to an Accelerated Rehabilitative Disposition or other probation without verdict program relative to any misdemeanor or felony offense under the laws of this Commonwealth or an equivalent offense under the laws of the United States or one of its territories or possessions, another state, the District of Columbia, the Commonwealth of Puerto Rico or a foreign nation; (iv) has not resigned a judicial commission to avoid having charges filed or to avoid prosecution by Federal, State or local law enforcement agencies or by the Judicial Conduct Board; (v) has not been removed from office by the Court of Judicial Discipline; and (vi) is a resident of this Commonwealth. (3) An active or senior judge or full-time magistrate of the District Courts of the United States for the Eastern, Middle or Western District of Pennsylvania. (3.1) An active, retired or senior bankruptcy judge of the United States Bankruptcy Courts for the Eastern, Middle or Western District of Pennsylvania who is a resident of this Commonwealth. (4) An active, retired or senior judge of the United States Court of Appeals for the Third Circuit who is a resident of this Commonwealth. (5) A mayor of any city or borough of this Commonwealth. (5.1) A former mayor of a city or borough of this Commonwealth who: (i) has not been defeated for reelection; (ii) has not been convicted of, pleaded nolo contendere to or agreed to an Accelerated Rehabilitative

Disposition or other probation without verdict program relative to a misdemeanor or felony offense under the laws of this Commonwealth or an equivalent offense under the laws of the United States or any one of its possessions, another state, the District of Columbia, the Commonwealth of Puerto Rico or a foreign nation; (iii) has not resigned the position of mayor to avoid having charges filed or to avoid prosecution by Federal, State or local law enforcement agencies; (iv) has served as a mayor, whether continuously or not, by election for an aggregate of a full term in office; and (v) is a resident of this Commonwealth. (6) A minister, priest or rabbi of any regularly established church or congregation. (b) Religious organizations. Every religious society, religious institution or religious organization in this Commonwealth may join persons together in marriage when at least one of the persons is a member of the society, institution or organization, according to the rules and customs of the society, institution or organization. (c) Marriage license needed to officiate. No person or religious organization qualified to perform marriages shall officiate at a marriage ceremony without the parties having obtained a marriage license issued under this part.

Rhode Island General Laws - Title 15: Domestic Relations - Chapter 15-3: Solemnization of Marriage § 15-3-5

Every ordained clergy or elder in good standing, every justice of the supreme court, superior court, family court, workers' compensation court, district court or traffic tribunal, the clerk of the supreme court, every clerk or general chief clerk of a superior court, family court, district court, or traffic tribunal, magistrates, special or general magistrates of the superior court, family court, traffic tribunal or district court, administrative clerks of the district court, administrators of the workers' compensation court, every former justice or judge and former administrator of these courts and every former chief clerk of the district court, and every former clerk or general chief clerk of a superior court, the secretary of the senate, elected clerks of the general assembly, any former secretary of the senate or any former elected clerk of the general assembly who retires after July 1, 2007, judges of the United States appointed pursuant to Article III of the United States Constitution, bankruptcy judges appointed pursuant to Article I of the United States Constitution, and United States magistrate judges appointed pursuant to federal law, may join persons in marriage in any city or town in this state; and every justice and every former justice of the municipal courts of the cities and towns in this state and of the police court of the town of Johnston and every probate judge and every former probate judge may join persons in marriage in any city or town in this state, and wardens of the town of New Shoreham may join persons in marriage in New Shoreham.

South Carolina Code of Laws - Title 20: Domestic Relations - Chapter 1: Marriage - Article 1: General Provisions § 20-1-20

Only ministers of the Gospel, Jewish rabbis, officers authorized to administer oaths in this State, and the chief or spiritual leader of a Native American Indian entity recognized by the

South Carolina Commission for Minority Affairs pursuant to Section 1-31-40 are authorized to administer a marriage ceremony in this State.

South Dakota Codified Laws - Title 25: Domestic Regulations - Chapter 1: Validity and Performance of Marriages § 25-1-30

Marriage may be solemnized by a justice of the Supreme Court, a judge of the circuit court, a magistrate, a mayor, either within or without the corporate limits of the municipality from which the mayor was elected, or any person authorized by a church to solemnize marriages.

Tennessee Code - Title 36: Domestic Relations - Chapter 3: Marriage - Part 3: Ceremony § 36-3-301

(a) (1) All regular ministers, preachers, pastors, priests, rabbis and other spiritual leaders of every religious belief, more than eighteen (18) years of age, having the care of souls, and all members of the county legislative bodies, county mayors, judges, chancellors, former chancellors and former judges of this state, former county executives or county mayors of this state, former members of quarterly county courts or county commissions, the governor, the speaker of the senate and former speakers of the senate, the speaker of the house of representatives and former speakers of the house of representatives, the county clerk of each county and the mayor of any municipality in the state may solemnize the rite of

North Shore Universal Church

matrimony. For the purposes of this section, the several judges of the United States courts, including United States magistrates and United States bankruptcy judges, who are citizens of Tennessee are deemed to be judges of this state. The amendments to this section by Acts 1987, ch. 336, which applied provisions of this section to certain former judges, do not apply to any judge who has been convicted of a felony or who has been removed from office. (2) In order to solemnize the rite of matrimony, any such minister, preacher, pastor, priest, rabbi or other spiritual leader must be ordained or otherwise designated in conformity with the customs of a church, temple or other religious group or organization; and such customs must provide for such ordination or designation by a considered, deliberate, and responsible act. (3) If any marriage has been entered into by license issued pursuant to this chapter at which any minister officiated before June 1, 1999, such marriage shall not be invalid because the requirements of the preceding subdivision (2) have not been met. (b) The traditional marriage rite of the Religious Society of Friends (Quakers), whereby the parties simply pledge their vows one to another in the presence of the congregation, constitutes an equally effective solemnization. (c) Any gratuity received by a county mayor, county clerk or municipal mayor for the solemnization of a marriage, whether performed during or after such person's regular working hours, shall be retained by such person as personal renumeration for such services, in addition to any other sources of compensation such person might receive, and such gratuity shall not be paid into the county general fund or the treasury of such municipality. (d) If any marriage has been entered into by license regularly issued at which a county executive officiated prior to April 24, 1981, such marriage shall be valid and is hereby declared to be in full compliance with the laws of this state. (e) For the purposes of this section, 'retired judges of this state' is construed to include persons who served as judges of any municipal or county court in any county that has adopted a metropolitan form of government and persons who served as county judges (judges of the quarterly county court) prior to the 1978 constitutional amendments. (f) If any marriage has been entered into by license regularly issued at which a retired judge of this state officiated prior to April 13, 1984, such marriage shall be valid and is hereby declared to be in full compliance with the laws of this state. (g) If any marriage has been entered into by license issued pursuant to this chapter at which a judicial commissioner officiated prior to March 28, 1991, such marriage is valid and is declared to be in full compliance with the laws of this state. (h) The judge of the general sessions court of any county, and any former judge of any general sessions court, may solemnize the rite of matrimony in any county of this state. Any marriage performed by any judge of the general sessions court in any county of this state before March 16, 1994, shall be valid and declared to be in full compliance with the laws of this state. (i) All elected officials and former officials, who are authorized to solemnize the rite of matrimony pursuant to the provisions of subsection (a), may solemnize the rite of matrimony in any county of this state. (j) If any marriage has been entered into by license issued pursuant to this chapter at which a county mayor officiated outside such mayor's county prior to May 29, 1997, such marriage is valid and is declared to be in full compliance with the laws of this state.

𝔑ort𝔥 𝔖𝔥ore 𝔘niversal 𝔆𝔥urc𝔥

Texas Statutes - Family Code - Title 1. The Marriage Relationship - Subtitle A. Marriage - Chapter 2. Subchapter C. Ceremony and Return of License § Sec. 2.202

(a) The following persons are authorized to conduct a marriage ceremony: (1) a licensed or ordained Christian minister or priest; (2) a Jewish rabbi; (3) a person who is an officer of a religious organization and who is authorized by the organization to conduct a marriage ceremony; and (4) a justice of the supreme court, judge of the court of criminal appeals, justice of the courts of appeals, judge of the district, county, and probate courts, judge of the county courts at law, judge of the courts of domestic relations, judge of the juvenile courts, retired justice or judge of those courts, justice of the peace, retired justice of the peace, judge of a municipal court, or judge or magistrate of a federal court of this state. (b) For the purposes of this section, a retired judge or justice is a former judge or justice who is vested in the Judicial Retirement System of Texas Plan One or the Judicial Retirement System of Texas Plan Two or who has an aggregate of at least 12 years of service as judge or justice of any type listed in Subsection (a)(4). (c) Except as provided by Subsection (d), a person commits an offense if the person knowingly conducts a marriage ceremony without authorization under this section. An offense under this subsection is a Class A misdemeanor. (d) A person commits an offense if the person knowingly conducts a marriage ceremony of a minor whose marriage is prohibited by law or of a person who by marrying commits an offense under Section 25.01, Penal Code. An offense under this subsection is a felony of the third degree.

Utah Code - Title 30: Husband and Wife - Chapter 1: Marriage § 30-1-6

(1) Marriages may be solemnized by the following persons only: (a) ministers, rabbis, or priests of any religious denomination who are: (i) in regular communion with any religious society; and (ii) 18 years of age or older; (b) Native American spiritual advisors; (c) the governor; (d) the lieutenant governor; (e) mayors of municipalities or county executives; (f) a justice, judge, or commissioner of a court of record; (g) a judge of a court not of record of the state; (h) judges or magistrates of the United States; (i) the county clerk of any county in the state, if the clerk chooses to solemnize marriages; (j) the president of the Senate; (k) the speaker of the House of Representatives; or (l) a judge or magistrate who holds office in Utah when retired, under rules set by the Supreme Court. (2) A person authorized under Subsection (1) who solemnizes a marriage shall give to the couple married a certificate of marriage that shows the: (a) name of the county from which the license is issued; and (b) date of the license's issuance. (3) As used in this section: (a) "Judge or magistrate of the United States" means: (i) a justice of the United States Supreme Court; (ii) a judge of a court of appeals; (iii) a judge of a district court; (iv) a judge of any court created by an act of Congress the judges of which are entitled to hold office during good behavior; (v) a judge of a bankruptcy court; (vi) a judge of a tax court; or (vii) a United States magistrate. (b) (i) "Native American spiritual advisor" means a person who: (A) (I) leads, instructs, or facilitates a Native American religious ceremony or service; or (II) provides religious counseling; and (B) is recognized as a spiritual advisor by a federally recognized Native American tribe. (ii) "Native American spiritual advisor"

includes a sweat lodge leader, medicine person, traditional religious practitioner, or holy man or woman. (4) Notwithstanding any other provision in law, no person authorized under Subsection (1) to solemnize a marriage may delegate or deputize another person to perform the function of solemnizing a marriage, except that only employees of the office responsible for the issuance of marriage licenses may be deputized.

Vermont Statutes - Title 18: Health - Part 6: Births, Marriages and Deaths - Chapter 105: Marriage Records and Licenses § § 5144

(a) Marriages may be solemnized by a supreme court justice, a superior judge, a judge of probate, an assistant judge, a justice of the peace, a magistrate, an individual who has registered as an officiant with the Vermont secretary of state pursuant to section 5144a of this title, a member of the clergy residing in this state and ordained or licensed, or otherwise regularly authorized thereunto by the published laws or discipline of the general conference, convention, or other authority of his or her faith or denomination, or by such a clergy person residing in an adjoining state or country, whose parish, church, temple, mosque, or other religious organization lies wholly or in part in this state, or by a member of the clergy residing in some other state of the United States or in the Dominion of Canada, provided he or she has first secured from the probate division of the superior court in the unit within which the marriage is to be solemnized a special authorization, authorizing him or her to certify the marriage if the probate judge determines that the circumstances make the special authorization desirable. Marriage among the Friends or Quakers, the Christadelphian Ecclesia, and the Baha'i Faith may be solemnized in the manner heretofore used in such societies. (b) This section does not require a member of the clergy authorized to solemnize a marriage as set forth in subsection (a) of this section, nor societies of Friends or Quakers, the Christadelphian Ecclesia, or the Baha'i Faith to solemnize any marriage, and any refusal to do so shall not create any civil claim or cause of action.

Code of Virginia - Title 20: Domestic Relations - Chapter 2: Marriage Generally § 20-37.1

All marriages heretofore solemnized outside this Commonwealth by a minister authorized to celebrate the rites of marriage in this Commonwealth, under a license issued in this Commonwealth, and showing on the application therefor the place out of this Commonwealth where said marriage is to be performed, shall be valid as if such marriage had been performed in this Commonwealth.

20-23. Order authorizing ministers to perform ceremony. When a minister of any religious denomination shall produce before the circuit court of any county or city in this Commonwealth, or before the judge of such court or before the clerk of such court at any time, proof of his ordination and of his being in regular communion with the religious society of which he is a reputed member, or proof that he holds a local minister's license and is serving as a regularly appointed pastor in his denomination, such court, or the judge thereof, or the clerk of such court at any time, may make an order authorizing such minister to celebrate the rites of matrimony in this Commonwealth. Any order made under this section may be rescinded at any time by the court or by the judge thereof.

Revised Code of Washington - Title 26: Domestic Relations - Chapter 4: Marriage § RCW 26.04.050

The following named officers and persons, active or retired, are hereby authorized to solemnize marriages, to wit: Justices of the supreme court, judges of the court of appeals, judges of the superior courts, supreme court commissioners, court of appeals commissioners, superior court commissioners, any regularly licensed or ordained minister or any priest of any church or religious denomination, and judges of courts of limited jurisdiction as defined in RCW 3.02.010.

Washington DC Code - Title 46: Domestic Relations - Subtitle 1: General - Chapter 4: Marriage § 46-406

(a) For the purposes of this section, the term: (1) 'Religious' includes or pertains to a belief in a theological doctrine, a belief in and worship of a divine ruling power, a recognition of a supernatural power controlling man's destiny, or a devotion to some principle, strict fidelity or faithfulness, conscientiousness, pious affection, or attachment. (2) 'Society' means a voluntary association of individuals for religious purposes. (b) For the purpose of preserving the evidence of marriages in the District of Columbia, every minister of any religious society approved or ordained according to the ceremonies of his religious society, whether his residence is in the District of Columbia or elsewhere in the United States or the territories, may be authorized by any judge of the Superior Court of the District of Columbia to celebrate marriages in the District of Columbia. Marriages may also be performed by any judge or justice of any court of record; provided, that marriages of any religious society which does not by its own custom require the intervention of a minister for the celebration of marriages may be solemnized in the manner prescribed and practiced in any such religious society, the license in such case to be issued to, and returns to be made by, a person appointed by such religious society for that purpose. The Clerk of the Superior Court of the District of Columbia or such deputy clerks of the Court as may, in writing, be designated by the Clerk and approved by the Chief Judge, may celebrate marriages in the District of Columbia. (c) No priest, imam, rabbi, minister, or other official of any religious society who is authorized to solemnize or celebrate marriages shall be required to solemnize or celebrate any marriage. (d) Each religious society has exclusive control over its own theological doctrine, teachings, and beliefs regarding who may marry within that particular religious society's faith. (e)(1) Notwithstanding any other provision of law, a religious society, or a nonprofit organization that is operated, supervised, or controlled by or in conjunction with a religious society, shall not be required to provide services, accommodations, facilities, or goods for a purpose related to the solemnization or celebration of a marriage, or the promotion of marriage through religious programs, counseling, courses, or retreats, that is in violation of the religious society's beliefs. (2) A refusal to provide services, accommodations, facilities, or goods in accordance with this subsection shall not create any civil claim or cause of action, or result in a District action to penalize or withhold benefits from the religious society or nonprofit organization that is operated, supervised, or controlled by or in conjunction with a religious society.

West Virginia Code - Chapter 48: Domestic Relations - Article 2: Marriages - Part 4: Marriage Ceremony § 48-2-401

A religious representative who has complied with the provisions of section 2-402, a family court judge, a circuit judge or a justice of the supreme court of appeals, is authorized to celebrate the rites of marriage in any county of this state. Celebration or solemnization of a marriage means the performance of the formal act or ceremony by which a man and woman contract marriage and assume the status of husband and wife. For purposes of this chapter, the term "religious representative" means a minister, priest or rabbi and includes, without being limited to, a leader or representative of a generally recognized spiritual assembly, church or religious organization which does not formally designate or recognize persons as ministers, priests or rabbis.

48-2-402. Qualifications of religious representative for celebrating marriages; registry of persons authorized to perform marriage ceremonies; special revenue fund. (a) Beginning the first day of September, two thousand one, the secretary of state shall, upon payment of the registration fee established by the secretary of state pursuant to subsection (d) of this section, make an order authorizing a person who is a religious representative to celebrate the rites of marriage in all the counties of the state, upon proof that the person: (1) Is eighteen years of age or older; (2) Is duly authorized to perform marriages by his or her church, synagogue, spiritual assembly or religious organization; and (3) Is in regular communion with the church, synagogue, spiritual assembly or religious organization of which he or she is a member. (b) The person shall give bond in the penalty of one thousand five hundred dollars, with surety approved by the commission. Any religious representative who gives proof before the county commission of his or her ordination or authorization by his or her respective church, synagogue, spiritual assembly or religious organization is exempt from giving the bond. (c) The secretary of state shall establish a central registry of persons authorized to celebrate marriages in this state. Every person authorized under the provisions of subsection (a) of this section to celebrate marriages shall be listed in this registry. Every county clerk shall, prior to the first day of October, two thousand one, transmit to the secretary of state the name of every person authorized to celebrate marriages by order issued in his or her county since one thousand nine hundred sixty and the secretary of state shall include these names in the registry. The completed registry and periodic updates shall be transmitted to every county clerk. (d) A fee not to exceed twenty-five dollars may be charged by the secretary of state for each registration received on or after the first day of September, two thousand one, and all money received shall be deposited in a special revenue revolving fund designated the "Marriage Celebrants Registration Fee Administration Fund" in the state treasury to be administered by the secretary of state. Expenses incurred by the secretary in the implementation and operation of the registry program shall be paid from the fund.

(e) No marriage performed by a person authorized by law to celebrate marriages may be invalidated solely because the person was not listed in the registry provided for in this section. (f) The secretary of state shall promulgate rules to implement the provisions of this section.

Wisconsin Statutes

Wisconsin Statutes - The Family - Chapter 765: Marriage § 765.16

Marriage may be validly solemnized and contracted in this state only after a marriage license has been issued therefor, and only by the mutual declarations of the 2 parties to be joined in marriage that they take each other as husband and wife, made before an authorized officiating person and in the presence of at least 2 competent adult witnesses other than the officiating person. The following are authorized to be officiating persons: (1) Any ordained member of the clergy of any religious denomination or society who continues to be an ordained member of the clergy. (2) Any licentiate of a denominational body or an appointee of any bishop serving as the regular member of the clergy of any church of the denomination to which the member of the clergy belongs, if not restrained from so doing by the discipline of the church or denomination. (3) The 2 parties themselves, by mutual declarations that they take each other as husband and wife, in accordance with the customs, rules and regulations of any religious society, denomination or sect to which either of the parties may belong. (4) Any judge of a court of record or a reserve judge appointed under s. 753.075. (5) Any circuit court commissioner appointed under SCR 75.02 (1) or supplemental court commissioner appointed under s. 757.675 (1). (6) Any municipal court judge.

765.17 Nonresident officiating person; sponsorship. Any member of the clergy, licentiate or appointee named in s. 765.16 who is not a resident of this state may solemnize marriages in this state if he or she possesses at the time of the marriage a letter of sponsorship from a member of the clergy of the same religious denomination or society who has a church in this state under his or her ministry.

765.19 Delivery and filing of marriage document. The marriage document, legibly and completely filled out with unfading black ink, shall be returned by the officiating person, or, in the case of a marriage ceremony performed without an officiating person, then by the parties to the marriage contract, or either of them, to the register of deeds of the county in which the marriage was performed within 3 days after the date of the marriage.

Wyoming Code

Wyoming Code - Title 20: Domestic Relations - Chapter 1: Husband and Wife - Article 1: Creation of Marriage § § 20-1-106

(a) Every district or circuit court judge, district court commissioner, supreme court justice, magistrate and every licensed or ordained minister of the gospel, bishop, priest or rabbi, or other qualified person acting in accordance with the traditions or rites for the solemnization of marriage of any religion, denomination or religious society, may perform the ceremony of marriage in this state. (b) In the solemnization of marriage, no particular form is required, except that the parties shall solemnly declare in the presence of the person performing the ceremony and at least two (2) attending witnesses that they take each other as husband and wife.

~ Notes ~

North Shore Universal Church

Wedding Officiant Manual

Made in the USA
Columbia, SC
06 May 2021